The

Evolution

of the

American Public High School

LYLE E. SCHALLER

The
Evolution
of the
American Public
High School

From Prep School to Prison
to New Partnerships

ABINGDON PRESS/ **Nashville**

THE EVOLUTION OF THE AMERICAN PUBLIC HIGH SCHOOL:
FROM PREP SCHOOL TO PRISON TO NEW PARTNERSHIPS

Copyright © 2000 by Abingdon Press

This book is printed on recycled, acid-free, elemental-chlorine–free paper.

Library of Congress Cataloging-in-Publication Data

Schaller, Lyle E.
  The evolution of the American public high school: from prep school to prison to new partnerships/by Lyle E. Schaller.
    p.   cm.
  ISBN 0-687-09840-8 (alk. paper)
    1. Education, Secondary—United States.   2. Public schools—United States.
  I. Title.

LB1607.5 .S34 2000
373.73—dc21

00-029985

00 01 02 03 04 05 06 07 08 09 — 10 9 8 7 6 5 4 3 2 1

MANUFACTURED IN THE UNITED STATES OF AMERICA

To

Jacob Nathaniel

Clara Elizabeth

Nicholas John

Henry Woods

George Thomas

Contents

Introduction

The first public high school in the United States was founded in Boston in 1821, but for all practical purposes the public high school in America was a creation of the last decade or two of the nineteenth century. One hundred years later most of the large public high schools had become dysfunctional institutions.

One reason for that growing number of large public high schools was that in the 1930–80 era, the legislatures in most states were persuaded to provide financial incentives to encourage the creation of large schools, including the elementary and middle grades as well as large high schools. By the mid-1960s it had become apparent that the heart of this debate was over criteria. The criteria used by most of the professional educators supported the trend toward big schools. Bigger is better! The criteria based on the welfare of the students supported those favoring small schools. Smaller really is better! That debate is far from resolved today.

In the year 2000 nearly 14 million adolescents were enrolled in grades 9 to 12 in approximately 20,000 public secondary schools. (These numbers exclude 5,300 special education schools, those that enroll grades 6-12, and alternative schools with a combined enrollment of 1.2 million.) One-fourth of those 20,000 schools reported an enrollment of 1,000 or more. Another 30 percent reported an enrollment of 500 to 999. Slightly over one-half (55 percent) of the secondary schools accounted for 78 percent of the enrollment. The remaining 22 percent of the enrollment, or 3 million students, was scattered among the 7,500 smaller public secondary schools.

The focus of this book is on the big public high schools with an enrollment of 800 or more. These are the one-third of the public high schools that include two-thirds of the students in grades 9-12. At the extreme end of the size spectrum, the approximately 900 very large public high schools with an enrollment of 2,000 or more account for one out of six students in grades 9-12 or 10-12.

Why have these large public high schools naturally tended to evolve into dysfunctional institutions? That is the theme of chapter 6.

What Are Your Assumptions?

Agreement on the health of any large tax-supported institution organized to provide person-centered services must begin with an agreement on assumptions about contemporary reality. The reader brings a set of assumptions to a book such as this one. The author owes that reader a statement of the assumptions being brought to this discussion. In order of importance, these are the critical assumptions on which this book is based:

1. The students represent the number-one constituency of today's public high schools. A complete list of constituents would inclu⌐ ⌐achers, administrators, parents, taxpayers, employers, ⌐nd university teachers and admissions counselo⌐ school board members, counselors, mayor⌐ ⌐stodians, secretaries, aides, officers of teach⌐ ⌐ legislators, governors, parole supervi-sor⌐ ⌐ workers, and others.

> **⌐s represent the number-one constituency public high schools.**

⌐ey assumption in this book, however, is that students ⌐tute the number-one constituency. Anyone disagreeing ⌐n that central assumption will have difficulty with much of ⌐ne content of the last several chapters. A persuasive argument can be made that this basic assumption is obsolete, idealistic, naive, or unrealistic, but it remains the key foundation stone for this book.

2. The ecological, physical, social, cultural, and economic

environment in which human beings exist influences our behavior.

The massacre at Columbine High School in Littleton, Colorado, in April 1999 generated a national debate. One slice of that debate focused on "Who's to blame?" The nominees included the easy access to firearms, students, motion pictures, television, video games, contemporary American society, the school board, teachers, administrators, parents, public safety officials, counselors, newspapers, teacher-training institutions, magazines, cliques, athletes, organized religion, the absence of a dress code, the lack of metal detectors at entrances into the building, the design of the building, and the alleged excessive caution displayed by the SWAT teams.

Almost completely absent from that discussion was this issue of the influence of the social setting or environment on the behavior of individuals.

That is the theme of the fourth chapter in this book. The basic thesis is the larger the number of people in that social setting and the greater the level of anonymity among the people, the more likely it is that some will engage in aberrant or antisocial behavior. The large mob is more dangerous than the small mob.

Systems produce what systems are designed to produce. The system now in place in most of the large public high schools in the United States is designed, unintentionally, of course, to produce alienation, boredom, adversarial relationships, disruptive behavior, and failure.

3. One's perception of reality is far more influential in determining behavior patterns than actual reality.

Motorists lock their vehicle when leaving it in what they perceive to be an unsafe location and leave it unlocked in what they perceive to be a safe location.

The public schools in the United States are remarkably safe places today, but in 1999 unprecedented sums of public funds were spent on the perception that they were unsafe.

Do high school students react to the environment in which they find themselves? Yes. But they are influenced to a far greater degree by their perception of that environment!

13

Introduction

In conversations with more than two thousand high school students, I have been impressed by the analogies they chose to describe their school. Those who describe it as a learning community tend to think and act as if they are members of a learning community. Those who compare it with a factory tend to describe it as a boring environment that causes people to look forward eagerly to the end of the workday and to the coming weekend. Those who use a prison as their analogy naturally tend to perceive their school as a hostile and controlled environment in which the paid staff are the controllers.

In other words, I believe the students' perception of their school environment is more likely to influence their behavior than the perception of that same environment held by a principal or a school board member or a teacher or a parent or a taxpayer.

The students' perception of their school environment is more likely to influence their behavior than the perception of that same environment held by a principal or a school board member or a teacher or a parent or a taxpayer.

---

4. One reasonable criterion for the evaluation of any institution designed to produce person-centered services is the impact on the next generation. Does the practice of medicine motivate the children of physicians to want to go to medical school? Does the practice of ministry motivate teenagers in that congregation to want to prepare for the parish ministry? Do the young patients of nurses want to enter that profession? Are the teenagers in the large public school today motivated by their experience to want to become high school teachers?

One of the major contemporary public policy issues is to decide who will be the classroom teachers in the year 2025. One answer to that question is that it is easier to recruit adults to serve as prison guards than it is to find adults who perceive high school teaching to be a rewarding and fulfilling career.

14

Introduction

All that is required to increase the inventory of potential factory workers or prison guards is to increase the dollar value of the compensation package.

If, however, the goal is to enlist teachers like Helen Highwater or Carl Swanson (who are described in chapter 12), the focus must be on creating a challenging and exciting learning environment that is a source of joy and satisfaction for both teenagers and teachers. The most effective way to assure a surplus of extremely competent high school teachers in 2025 is for the ecological environment of the public high school of 2010 to produce these two reactions among the people in that school.

> **The focus must be on creating a challenging and exciting learning environment that is a source of joy and satisfaction for both teenagers and teachers.**

The first is an ecological environment that motivates every teacher (or at least every teacher with five or more years of experience) to model this image: "The wisest vocational decision I ever made was to become a teacher! Every weekend I look forward to Monday morning. Every summer I look forward to when school reopens. I love what I'm doing! Some days I even feel a little guilty about being paid to do this. I was taught that work is difficult, hard, and burdensome. That is why workers need their weekends free and regular vacations from their job. I love my work! Teaching in this high school is fun. The only cloud on the horizon is, I suppose, that someday I will be forced to retire, but I try not to think about that."

That is not an image conveyed by most factory workers or prison guards. It is an image that is projected by adults who are convinced that they are following their calling and are serving in an ecological environment that is supportive of their gifts, their skills, their commitment, their idealism, their dreams, and their vocational choice.

Introduction

While it is true that some of today's unhappy and frustrated high school teachers are victims of an unwise career choice, this observer is convinced that most of them are victims of a system designed to produce frustration, unhappiness, and failure.

Some of today's unhappy and frustrated high school teachers are victims of an unwise career choice . . . most of them are victims of a system designed to produce frustration, unhappiness, and failure.

The second desired reaction is an ecological environment that motivates perhaps 5 percent of the best students in every class to conclude, "I would love to spend the rest of my life in this social setting with my peers and my teachers. I have discovered a joy in learning here and have been inspired by so many teachers who display that joy in learning that I want to be a high school teacher. I see more good models of what it means to be a healthy, happy, and useful adult here than I see anywhere else in my life."

In other words, a basic assumption in this book is that the beginning point for providing a plentiful supply of competent, committed, and enthusiastic high school teachers in 2025 is to transform the factory or prison model into a challenging learning community.

5. It is much easier to create the new than it is to reform the old! If the public policy makers of 2001 agree that the large public high school has become a dysfunctional institution, one alternative is to begin to reform and restructure the ecological environment of those 11,000 public high schools with an enrollment over 600. Together they account for 80 percent of the combined enrollment. A reasonable timeframe would call for completion of that effort by 2040 or 2050. Among other price tags on such a schedule will be a continued shortage of committed and competent teachers for at least a half century.

Introduction

A realistic alternative would be to focus that reform and redesign effort on the one-third of all large public high schools that have moved out of the denial stage of their institutional journey and concurrently begin to create new models of a public high school designed to be challenging and effective learning communities to accommodate the majority of that passing parade of high school students.

A fringe benefit of this more aggressive strategy is that competition is a useful motivator of reform and innovation.

6. For more than a century, much of the public discussion on the role of the high school has focused on two questions. First, what should be taught? Should it be a precollege curriculum? Or vocational training? Or should it equip graduates to be productive and active citizens in a democratic society? Second, how should that curriculum be taught? By memorizing a common core of facts? Or by training students to reflect and analyze? Or by mastering skills needed in the labor market?

A core assumption here is that this discussion should include a third component. In addition to the "What?" and the "How?" this discussion should include the issue of "Where?" The cultural, pedagogical, physical, and social setting or environment for learning also teaches. The central thesis of this book is that the typical large public high school provides an ecological environment for learning that often ranges between negative and hostile. This is the theme of chapters 1, 3, 4, 6, 10, and 12.

> **The typical large public high school provides an ecological environment for learning that often ranges between negative and hostile.**

7. If the public secondary schools have been created to serve as educational centers in which adolescents experience the joy of learning, as allies to help parents socialize teenagers into the American culture, as learning communities to prepare students for admission into college or university, as trade schools to

equip graduates to enter the paid labor force as contributing workers, and as partners to help parents rear their children, then the large public high school merits a grade of A or B with no more than 40 percent of the students, perhaps a C with another 25 percent, and a grade of D or lower with at least one-third of the students.

What is the acceptable level of success required to continue allocating $100 billion annually to operate public high schools? Do taxpayers have a right to expect that four years in high school will be a productive and valuable experience for 90 percent of the students? Or 80 percent? Or 75 percent? Or 65 percent? Or 50 percent? Or only 40 percent?

While four years represents only 5 or 6 percent of the total life span for most adults, for eighteen-year-olds it is close to a quarter of their lives to date. What is a good investment of those four years?

8. The students and the classroom teachers are not the sources of the problems plaguing many of today's larger public high schools. The students and the classroom teachers are the primary victims of dysfunctional systems. That is a major theme of chapters 4, 6, 10, and 12.

9. In today's world we recognize the natural tendency of systems to produce what they are designed to produce. We also have accumulated the reservoir of experience, knowledge, wisdom, and skills required to diagnose the shortcomings of the dysfunctional system, and we know how to respond creatively to the dysfunctional system. That is the theme of chapter 8.

10. The pedagogical design of most public high schools is controlled by college- and university-educated adults who were taught that the normative learning environment consists of a classroom with one instructor and a desk or table in front of a wall that can be used for writing. The room also contains a number of chairs facing that wall, each with one wide arm for writing. The basic channel for communication consists of words, either spoken or printed, such as this page in this book. Most of the session is devoted to the instructor's talking and the students' taking notes. That process may be interrupted

occasionally by questions from a student or by the instructor's directing a question to a student.

Most of the children born in the United States in 1985 and later have been taught by our culture that the most effective learning environments are organized around (a) field trips or (b) experiential events such as competitive interscholastic athletic games or publishing a school newspaper or involvement in community service or an active role as a member of a debate team or (c) a visit to a new interactive "hands-on" science museum or (d) music or (e) watching moving images on a motion picture or television screen or (f) an interactive relationship with a computer or (g) peer led and controlled experiences such as "hanging out together at the mall" or serving as a juror or prosecutor in a teen court or working together as a team on a science project.

The child born in 1985 or later comes to high school today with an early twenty-first-century understanding of an effective learning environment. The typical high school is designed, both pedagogically and architecturally, to provide an up-to-date model of a 1935 learning environment (chapter 12 describes a potential model for 2005.)

The natural, normal, and predictable consequences of this dysfunctional system are discontent, conflict, and alienation.

11. The societal context for formal education at all ages and levels changed dramatically during the last few decades of the twentieth century. That is the theme of the seventh chapter. The public high school in the early decades of the twenty-first century must be designed to function in a different pedagogical and societal context from what prevailed in the 1930s or even the 1960s.

12. Most public high school districts or service areas are defined in geographical terms. Enrollment in a particular high school usually is determined by the student's place of residence. This is consistent with the pre-World War II concept of geographically defined neighborhoods. As Peter Drucker has pointed out, modern means of transportation have removed many of the old barriers that limited mobility.[1] (One example of the

growing irrelevance of geographical distance is the rapidly increasing number of "virtual high schools" in cyberspace created by state governments or tax-funded colleges and universities. Many of these service students who reside in another state or even another country.)

The second half of this assumption is that today's teenagers, like their parents, tend to prefer self-selected social networks. The geographically defined parish in American Christianity is disappearing. Adults build their friendship circles from among people they meet at work or in a voluntary association or in recreational experiences or who are engaged in the same vocation. Like their parents, today's teenagers are comfortable with self-segregated patterns of interpersonal relationships.

This means the large public high school encompassing an area of twenty square miles that includes 3,000 persons of high school age has three choices. One is to service that population with four to ten schools, each with its own distinctive role and culture. Students in that district, regardless of place of residence or future career plans, would enroll in the school of their choice. A second option would be to give each student a tuition voucher to enroll in the school of that student's choice.

A third option is to compel all students, regardless of future career plans, who reside within the geographically defined boundaries of that one large public high school to enroll in that school or to pay their own tuition to a private school. The resulting discontent, conflict, and alienation should be accepted as a normal, natural, and predictable price tag that is part of any system of incarceration.

13. While it is not a part of the United States Constitution, it is assumed here that, sooner or later, the Declaration of Independence will become an influential reference point in determining how tax monies will be used for educational purposes in the twenty-first century. In more specific terms, that document declares, "We hold these truths to be self-evident, that all men are created equal . . . that among [their unalienable rights] are Life, Liberty and the Pursuit of Happiness. That . . . Governments . . . [derive] their just powers from the consent of

the governed. That whenever any form of Government becomes destructive of these ends it is the right of the People to alter or to abolish it. . . ."

When a majority of government-owned and operated institutions that are financed out of tax funds fail to meet widely accepted performance standards, do the people have the right to alter or abolish them? Does the right to the pursuit of life, liberty, and happiness include the right to a relevant, challenging, and high-quality educational experience?

This writer assumes that "the People"—parents, students, taxpayers, teachers, et al.—do possess an inherent right to abolish, replace, and/or alter the system of tax-funded public schools in the United States. Chapter 8 describes how this has been happening with the United States Postal System over the past seven decades. That government-owned and operated monopoly has had to adapt to competition. Will the government-owned and operated monopoly in secondary education be next?

14. The level of discontent with what is happening—and not happening—in the large public high school is rising. A growing number of parents, teachers, employers, students, taxpayers, and others are becoming increasingly disenchanted with the performance of the public schools in general and the large public high schools in particular.

Discontent with the status quo is the crucial component in the process of planned change.[2] Therefore, the most positive basis for hope for a better learning environment for the children born after 1985 is this rising level of discontent with today's public high school.

The purpose of this book is to provide grist for that mill of public discussion.

For those readers interested in an author's credentials, this writer (a) graduated from a one-teacher, eight-grade rural elementary school; (b) graduated from a tax-supported public high school; (c) married a woman who had graduated from a large public high school; (d) expected to teach in a public high school following graduation from the University of Wisconsin with a major in American history and all of the academic credentials from the School of Education required for certification as a high school teacher in Wisconsin, but instead chose a career in planning; (e) is the father of six children, all of whom graduated from large public high schools; (f) has enjoyed and benefited from extended conversations with over 2,000 high school students in forty-six states; (g) has spent fifty years working for, working with, studying, researching, writing about, and reporting on nonprofit institutions organized to deliver person-centered services; (h) instead of playing golf or tennis or bungee jumping or chasing women or going to the movies or sky diving as a hobby, long ago chose reading and writing; and (i) was persuaded in the early 1970s of the power of the social, physical, economic, demographical, pedagogical, religious, geographical, educational, and work environment on human behavior and has been chasing that rabbit for nearly three decades.

Every book I have written has been enriched by the contributions of others. This is not an exception! My primary debt is to a couple of thousand teenagers, parents, public school teachers, and administrators who have shared their experiences, frustrations, insights, reflections, wisdom, and learnings with me. Another big debt is to others who have written on this subject. A few of them are identified in the notes at the end of this volume.

I also am indebted to Sarah Brunker for her critical reading of an early version of the last chapter.

This book is dedicated to our five grandchildren who will be engaged in some form of secondary education in the 2004–17 era.

Chapter One

FROM PREP SCHOOL TO PRISON

Agriculture was the number-one occupation in the labor force of the American colonies in 1700. A distant second was the movement of cargo and passengers over water. Both occupations provided employment opportunities for teenage males.

At the Chicago World's Fair in 1893, a University of Wisconsin professor, Frederick Jackson Turner, read what was later recognized as one of the landmark pieces of historical research. Turner declared the American frontier had closed in 1890. That essay, "The Significance of the Frontier in American History," gave birth to a new school of thought in American history.[1]

Forty years earlier, Horace Greeley had begun to popularize the advice John Soule gave to the unemployed of New York City: "Go west, young man." The western frontier of the nineteenth century had provided challenging opportunities for the young men of that era, but now it was closed.

The tenth volume in the monumental series *A History of American Life* was written by Arthur M. Schlesinger, Sr., and published in 1933. The title was *The Rise of the City 1878–1898.*[2]

It is not a coincidence that the birth of the modern American public high school coincided with the closing of the frontier and the birth of the modern American city.

Farming, mining, seafaring, and forestry had provided a variety of opportunities for healthy, energetic, and ambitious teenage males to be tired by the end of a long workday. The old response to the question of what to do with aggressive young males was to put them to work. The cities did not provide the necessary quantity of jobs, especially for fourteen-, fifteen-, and sixteen-year-olds. The new answer in urban America was to warehouse them in a controlled environment called a public high school.

The professionals of the day, however, could not affirm that as an acceptable justification for the expenditure of public funds. They rephrased the issue around the "need for preparation" and chose sides over the central reason for funding public high schools.

Preparation for What?

The earliest public high schools were largely modeled after the privately financed college preparatory schools. What other models were out there to be copied? The next best model was the tax-supported common school.

This naturally led one group of schoolmen (to use a common label of that era) to urge that the public high school be perceived as the successor to the privately funded preparatory schools and academies, and prepare adolescents for admission to college. The other side contended that secondary education should prepare adolescents to become informed and active citizens in the democratic society. Therefore, the primary purpose of tax-supported high schools should be to prepare the students for life. One critic challenged the classical side with the question, "Do we prepare students for the twelfth or the twentieth century?"

The impact of recent history, educational traditions, and the value systems of the professionals was illustrated by the report prepared by the historic Committee of Ten. After years of debate over the issue, at a meeting of the National Educational Association (NEA) in 1892, the Committee of Ten was created. The ten included the president of Harvard University, the president of the University of Colorado (and former principal of the Denver High School), the presidents of three other colleges or universities (Vassar, Missouri, Michigan), the headmasters or principals of three eastern secondary schools, a college professor, and the Commissioner of Education for the United States (the former superintendent of public schools in St. Louis).

Their report was published in 1894. A recognition of the diversity of the constituency can be found in Table IV of that report. It described four "programmes" or courses of study. The one that was clearly a college preparatory sequence was labeled "Classical." It required four years of Latin plus two years of Greek, three years of German or French, four years of English plus four years of mathematics, a year of chemistry, a year of physics, two years of history, and a year of physical geography. The less rigorous "Latin-Scientific" curriculum called for only two foreign languages with Latin and English being four-year requirements. The "Modern Language" alternative required four years of English plus four years of either French or German and three years of the other.

At the other end of this spectrum was the curriculum to prepare students for life. It required only one foreign language and recommended it be Latin, German, or French with a four-year requirement for that one language. It also included four years of English, four years of history, four years of mathematics, and a combined total equal to seven years of science and geography.[3]

The report from this elite committee did not evoke universal approval. One criticism was that it overlooked the fact that it appeared to be directed at high schools with six to twelve teachers when the majority had only one or two.

Another criticism was based on the fact that in 1889–90 fewer than 10 percent of all students enrolled in secondary schools ever graduated. This was countered by the argument that the focus of the report of the Committee of Ten was on preparation for life, not preparation for college!

The Context

Recommendations on the role of the public high school should be evaluated in the context of the era in which they were formulated. In 1880, for example, the public high school ranked only fourth in enrollment on the American educational scene. In first place, of course, were the public elementary schools with an enrollment of nearly 9.8 million pupils. A distant second were the nonpublic elementary schools with an estimated enrollment of well over a half million, followed by the 116,000 enrolled as candidates for a degree in institutions of higher education. In fourth place, in terms of enrollment, were the 110,227 students, up sharply from 80,227 in 1871, enrolled in public high schools.

One operational assumption of the nineteenth century was that wealthy parents would enroll their children in college, while the rest of the parents sent their teenage children into the labor force.

Another widespread assumption was that secondary schools existed to prepare young people for college—and that was the primary role of the private secondary schools of that era.

A new and growing operational assumption was that younger teenagers needed to be warehoused only for a year or two before entering the labor force.

Did It Work?

More than three out of five of all high school graduates now enroll in an institution of higher education. That is up from 50 percent in 1965. They enroll in tax-supported community colleges, private colleges, tax-supported universities, and other types of schools. Does this suggest that high school has become primarily a college preparatory experience?

One response comes from scores of university professors who complain that their first-year students are deficient in communication skills (many come with transmitters but lack receivers), in numerical skills, and in being able to comprehend abstract concepts.

A more constructive response came from the College of Arts and Humanities at the University of Maryland. All incoming freshmen are required to take a two-credit course, "University 101." The content includes an introduction to the library, training students to come to class on time, an explanation of why students should not bring a meal to class and eat it during the lecture, how to write a coherent paragraph, why the chewing of gum in class is not an approved activity, and that "student rights" do not include the right to get up and walk out of class partway through the period.

That response illustrates the point that there is a limit to how much etiquette can be taught in a warehouse.

The most radical response came in 1998 from Baruch College in the City University of New York. The leaders began with the assumption that college-level work should be offered by that college. Therefore, only those candidates for admission who were capable of college-level study should be admitted. They eliminated all remedial courses. The former interim president of Baruch College subsequently concluded that "offering pre-college work in colleges and universities is a grievous error."[4]

If that radical point of view were universally adopted, it would have at least three politically unacceptable consequences:

1. It would sharply reduce the number of first-year students seeking to enroll in colleges and universities.

2. The resulting drop in enrollment would result in the loss of thousands of jobs for college and university teachers and administrators.

3. It would place unacceptably severe pressures on the high schools to prepare students for college-level work.

From 2 Percent to 80 Percent

A major reason for that national debate in the 1890s over the ideal high school curriculum was the sharp increase in enrollment and graduation rates that began after the Civil War and the subsequent emphasis on graduation. The number of students graduating from high school was 16,000 in 1870, a year in which the number entering first grade was over a million. The number of high school graduates doubled to 32,000 in 1883, doubled again to 65,000 in 1894, doubled again to 129,000 in

27

1908, doubled again to 1,068,000 in 1937, and doubled again to 2,290,000 in 1964. That 1964 number was 143 times the number of high school graduates of 96 years earlier! Since 1980, the number of students graduating from high school each year has ranged between the high of 2.9 million in 1980 and the low of 2.4 million in 1990, with the 1990s averaging 2.5 million annually.

In 1870 the number of teenagers graduating from high school was equal to 2.0 percent of the seventeen-year-olds in the American population. That proportion climbed to 2.5 percent in 1880 and 3.5 percent in 1890. It nearly doubled to 6.4 percent in 1900, reached 8.8 percent in 1910, nearly doubled to 16.8 percent in 1920, grew to 29.0 percent in 1930, passed the 50 percent level to 50.8 in 1940, jumped to 59 percent in 1950, and reached 80 percent in the 1990s.

The Need for More Warehouses

In 1921, for the first time in American history, the number of live births exceeded three million. That produced a record number of sixteen-year-olds in 1937. With the exception of 1919, live births in the United States ranged between 2.8 million and 3.1 million annually from 1911 through 1927. That "baby boom" was followed by a "birth dearth" from 1928 through 1941, when live births ranged from a low of 2.3 million in 1933 to a high of 2.7 million in 1941. (That earlier baby boom produced most of the American troops for World War II.)

When the children brought by immigrant parents before the cutback in immigration in 1931 were added to those births, the result was a huge number of teenagers and young adults in the population during the 1930s. Between 1920 and 1930 the annual influx of immigrants ranged from a high of 805,228 in 1921 to a low of 241,700 in 1930. That figure dropped to between 24,000 and 83,000 annually in the 1932–45 era.

The spread of state laws compelling full-time school attendance until age sixteen (thirty states had such laws by 1918)[5] combined with that unprecedented number of teenagers in the 1930s, plus the huge numbers of unemployed because of the Great Depression, created the need for more warehouses. One estimate was that youth aged 16-24 accounted for one-third of the unemployed. One proposal claimed that the national labor force could be reduced by 4.4 million by making high school graduation a universal requirement. One university professor urged that the custodial role of education be extended to age twenty-five.[6]

The first response by the federal government to this need for more custodial facilities was the Civilian Conservation Corps (CCC), which opened its first camp on April 17, 1933. Two years later the National Youth Administration (NYA), a pet project of Eleanor Roosevelt and Secretary of Labor Frances Perkins, was launched. State directors were given the responsibility for creating the appropriate program for their state. One of the very best was in Texas. It was the creation of a twenty-seven-year-old former teacher named Lyndon B. Johnson. In addition to providing financial subsidies for needy students, by 1940 the NYA also had established 600 "resident centers" that had a combined full-time enrollment of 30,000 young men and women. Both the NYA and the CCC had a central emphasis on education and job training.

Before long, both were widely viewed as threats to the traditional education establishment. Therefore, it was not surprising that the war in Europe provided a convenient excuse to terminate them.[7] The professional educators won that battle to control the warehouse.

What did those programs cost? A report published in 1941 stated that the average annual cost for eighteen- and nineteen-year-olds who enrolled in a public high school was $200. The $720 annual cost for each resident of an NYA residential center included $360 for wages. The average annual cost for each CCC worker was approximately $1,000, and that included $30 a month for wages.[8] Those numbers should be multiplied by eleven to adjust for the increase in the Consumer Price Index between 1938 and 2000.

The late nineteenth century introduced the idea of using the public high school to warehouse teenagers until they were old enough to enter the labor force. The twentieth century adopted that as the norm, with the brief exception of the 1930s in the battle over control of the warehouses. By the last decade of the twentieth century, the analogy of the public high school as a warehouse for restless and unemployed adolescents had been replaced, at least in the eyes of many students, by a new image.

A Contemporary Image

Two days after the April 1999 bloodbath at Columbine High School in suburban Denver, two bomb squad trucks rushed to another suburban Denver school in response to a warning that a backpack containing explosives had been found. A reporter was there to interview students as they streamed out of the building. A fifteen-year-old girl explained to the reporter, "It's like a prison in there!" "You can't even go to the bathroom without permission, and then they time you," another fifteen-year-old complained. "All the teachers now wear name tags, and there is an armed guard or a teacher at every door!"

* * * *

That same evening in a well-to-do suburban community 900 miles east of Denver, a father returned from a business trip and asked his sixteen-year-old daughter what the impact of the disaster in Littleton would have on her school. She replied, "It will be more like a prison than it is now. We'll have metal detectors at every entrance. Instead of the two we have now, we'll probably have five or six police officers on duty every day. Everyone will have to wear name tags, and there will be more surveillance cameras in the hallways, cafeteria, and classrooms."

"Why will everyone be required to wear a name tag?" asked the naive father.

"To make it easier for the police to identify the dead in case there is a shooting," replied the more sophisticated daughter.

* * * *

Five years earlier a sixteen-year-old girl from a public high school in Pennsylvania, along with a dozen other teenagers who attended suburban schools, was being interviewed. At one point in the conversation, she explained that frequently she missed her first-period class. "A lot of the kids hang out on the east side of the building to have a last minute smoke before school starts. If my bus is on time, I can get in ahead of them, but if the bus is a few minutes late, I'll be at the end of the line of kids waiting to go through the metal detectors. The teacher for my first-period class locks the door five minutes after the bell rings. If I'm at the end of the line, it takes fifteen to twenty minutes to get through the metal detectors, so I miss that first-period class."

"Sounds more like a prison than a school," commented a suburban boy.

"Yeah," replied the girl.

Why Do They Call It a Prison?

In the 1980s and early 1990s, "boring" was frequently used to describe school life. The new generation of students is more likely to use terms like "dangerous" and "fear." During the 1990s I met an increasing number of teenagers who used the analogy of a prison when describing their high school. A few were surprised when I challenged the validity of that analogy. Most of the explanations can be summarized in a few brief paragraphs.[9]

One fourteen-year-old freshman pointed out that criminals frequently are sentenced, as required by state law, to a term of one to five years in a tax-supported institution called a prison. He recalled that at age six he had been sentenced to a ten-year term in public schools. Since his parents could not afford to appeal that state-mandated sentence by enrolling him in a private school, he still had two years left to serve. He added that criminals can have their sentence shortened in return for good behavior. He complained that regardless of how well he behaved, he still had two years to serve on his ten-year sentence.

The reformers contend that prisons should focus on learning. Both prisons and public high schools have turned out to be far from universal success stories.

The Evolution of the American Public High School

A prison has armed guards on duty. Many of the large public high schools have armed police officers on duty.

Prisons occasionally experience an outbreak of deadly violence initiated by the inmates. Large public high schools occasionally experience an outbreak of deadly violence initiated by students. Similar outbreaks of violence rarely occur in shopping malls or retirement villages.

Paid staff in prisons are often threatened by the inmates, and occasionally paid staff persons are the victims of physical violence. Teachers in large public high schools report that they often are threatened by students, and some do become the victims of physical violence.

Someone seeking to visit a relative confined to prison must receive a pass to enter the building and be escorted to the meeting place. A relative seeking to visit a student in the large public high school usually has to secure permission to enter the building and often is escorted to the meeting place.

The well-connected prisoner often has access to weapons and drugs. The well-connected student usually has easy access to weapons and drugs.

It is not unusual to hold an unscheduled "shakedown" in the prison to discover contraband. It is increasingly common for officials to conduct an unannounced search of students' lockers to discover contraband.

It is not uncommon for a group of prison inmates to formulate, articulate, and enforce the unofficial norms for acceptable behavior by the other inmates. It is not unusual for a clique of high school students to formulate, disseminate, and enforce the unofficial norms for acceptable dress and behavior by the rest of the high school students.

At the bottom of the social pecking order in both prisons and high schools are those persons who have been identified as snitches.

In 1934 President Franklin D. Roosevelt persuaded officials of the American Federation of Labor not to oppose a proposal to allow federal prisoners to be engaged in paid labor. The reason for this proposal was a recent increase in the level of violence in the prisons. It was hoped that involvement in meaningful work would de-escalate the level of disturbances initiated by the inmates. It worked. In 1999 the Federal Prison Industries, a self-supporting agency within the United States Department of Justice, was employing 20,000 prisoners, up from 6,300 in 1980, who receive a nominal wage for producing goods and services. That total is expected to reach 30,000 by 2006. These workers declare it is a meaningful and often enjoyable experience when compared to simply sitting in a prison cell.[10]

A large proportion of sixteen-, seventeen-, and eighteen-year-old high school students work at part-time paid jobs during the school year. "Every one of us needs some kind of measureable feedback on how we're doing," I explain as I ask these students one of a series of questions. "Which provides the most meaningful feedback to how you're doing? Your high school report card or your paycheck from work?" The vast majority, often over 90 percent, raise their hands when I offer the paycheck alternative.

New inmates in a prison quickly discover which cliques or gangs are at the top of the status hierarchy in that particular institution. New students in the large public high school quickly discover which social networks or cliques are at the top of the status ladder in that particular institution and which tribes "own" that school.

The newly arrived inmate in a prison who is able to earn the acceptance of the members in the gang at the top of that deference pyramid usually can enjoy a relatively high degree of physical safety and also expect to receive the appropriate level of deference from the other inmates. The junior who moves into the community from another state in August and is able to earn quick acceptance from the members of the number-one clique in that large public school usually finds it easy to meet and make friends from among those lower on the deference pyramid.

In the typical prison, several paid staff members, regardless of title or tenure, have earned the respect of most of the inmates while others are described in scornful terms. In the large public high school several of the paid staff, regardless of title or tenure,

33

have earned the respect, and possibly even the admiration, of many students. Others are the objects of scorn.

This is not offered as a comprehensive set of parallels, but only as an effort to illustrate a student perspective.

Another Perspective

From an adult perspective, a few other parallels help to illustrate the same point.

Most prisoners are delighted to be allowed to leave on parole or to receive an unconditional discharge. By contrast, many adults go to the banquet to honor them on retirement and leave filled with regret that the calendar has forced them to enter a new stage in their life cycle. For most seventeen- and eighteen-year-olds, does high school graduation generate the feelings experienced by the person being released from prison or the adult retiring after many years with the same employer?

One alternative to serving that sentence in an overcrowded and dangerous prison is home confinement. One alternative to attending an overcrowded and dangerous large public high school is home schooling.

Three of the top priorities in the decision-making processes of the modern prison are (1) to provide a safe environment for every prisoner and every employee, (2) to rehabilitate prisoners to prepare them to lead socially acceptable and economically productive lives after they are released, and (3) to provide a warehouse for individuals who have been rejected by society and convicted by the criminal justice system.

Three of the top priorities in the large public high school today are (1) to provide a safe environment for students and employees, (2) to offer remedial instruction when needed to prepare students for meaningful participation in the classroom or in the labor force, (3) to provide a place to store adolescents until they are old enough to enter the labor force.

One solution to the problems of the contemporary prison system is to recruit a better class of convicts. They are sent to the medium-security prisons.

From Prep School to Prison

One solution to the problems of the contemporary public high school is to recruit a better class of students. They are enrolled in magnet schools.

The wealthy defendant convicted of a serious felony often can have a choice of the prisons operated at public expense. A Minnesota parent pointed out that every student can choose any public school in that state but must provide his or her own transportation, which can be expensive.

Syndicated columnist Steve Chapman pointed out that drug-testing of prison inmates has long been accepted, and drug testing of public high school students engaged in extracurricular activities also is becoming commonplace. Chapman went on to point out, "At school, you don't get cable TV. Otherwise the similarities grow more striking every day. Both house large numbers of people who are compelled to be there and are treated by their overseers as dangerous, incorrigible and undeserving of respect."[11]

You have been earning $175,000 a year, you have been happily married for seventeen years, and you are the father of a fifteen-year-old and a twelve-year-old daughter. A month before your fortieth birthday you are convicted of a serious white-collar felony. The sentence is five years in a federal penitentiary with parole possible after three years. What emotions flood over you as the sentence is pronounced? Number three may be the shame you have brought to your family. Number two may be what will happen to your wife and children. Number one probably will be fear for your physical safety when you enter the penitentiary. You've read the newspapers and magazine stories. You've watched television. Your wife and children also share your fear.

What is a common emotion among mothers as they send their children off to begin the first day of the first year in that large public high school? Or, increasingly, to enter middle school? What was the number-one emotion of many students who returned to Columbine High School in August 1999?

The answer, of course, is fear.

What are the alternatives? One is the minimum-security

prison for the middle-class felon. Another is the small private high school with a fairly homogeneous student body. American society has decided that everyone does not have to be treated equally.

Back in the years of the Great Depression, the 1930s, two characteristics of a "good job" were, "It's inside work" and "There is no heavy lifting."

What are the two most common criticisms of today's megachurches? The usual answer is anonymity and complexity.

What are two of the most common explanations for the continued existence of tens of thousands of small Protestant congregations? A frequent response is, "People enjoy the intimacy and the absence of complexity. Life is simpler in the small church."

What are two of the most common complaints of prisoners? Anonymity and life is controlled by the calendar and the clock.

What are two of the reasons given for leaving that large public high school to attend a small private (or public) high school? They left anonymity and a life that was run by the calendar and clock for the intimacy and spontaneity of the small school. (It is worth adding at this point that public policy in recent years has called for bigger prisons and larger public high schools, both of which generate a higher level of anonymity and a drift toward greater centralized control.)

Back in the 1930s a high school teacher ranked below the physician and above the nurse on the social ladder. In addition to its being inside work without any heavy lifting, teaching was a respected vocation. Most public high schools also were relatively uncomplicated social systems that encouraged one-to-one relationships among the teachers and also between a teacher and a promising student. In most public high schools of that day everyone could call nearly every student correctly by name. *Anonymity* was a word to be used in a spelling bee.

Today many public high school students see themselves as anonymous figures in a complex social setting. Students frequently complain that it takes several weeks before they learn the names of every student in their math class, and they do not even try to become acquainted with every student in the school. If given a choice, many people would prefer a daily environment filled with intimacy rather than anonymity.

In 1998, by a margin of four to three, the members of the local board of education voted not to renew the contract of the superintendent of a very large K–12 public school system. That decision generated a heated debate throughout that suburban community and received extensive coverage in the local newspapers. After a year of intense public discussion the conflict finally was resolved and the superintendent was reinstated in office. An informal poll of the students at the very large four-year public high school revealed that a majority of those interviewed, when given the name of the superintendent, could not identify that individual or explain why he was in the news. That incident illustrated the meaning of the word *anonymity.*

> **The road to safe schools and to creating challenging learning communities begins with changing the ecological environment.**

Finally, high school teachers today rank above warehouse employees and prison guards in the deference pyramid, but far below physicians and many other vocations.

One hundred years ago, in the 1890s, professional educators were divided over whether a public high school should be organized to prepare students for college or to prepare students for life.

In 1999 the big line of demarcation dividing professional educators and school board members into two groups was whether the focus should be on (1) making the large public high school a more secure and safe environment, like a good prison, or on (2) enhancing the sense of responsibility among the students and teachers to strengthen the self-identity as a learning community.

The national media devoted a disproportionately large

amount of coverage to those who favored creating safe prisons. That bias in the national media reinforced in the minds of students that a prison was an appropriate analogy to use in describing their high school.

The central thesis of this book is that both sides in that public debate overlook the most critical variable. The road to safe schools and to creating challenging learning communities begins with changing the ecological environment. Before chasing that rabbit, however, it may be useful to look at two other components of the context.

Chapter Two

A CENTURY OF EXPLOSIVE GROWTH

etween 1890 and 1990 the population of the United States quadrupled from 63 million to 250 million. The enrollment in public elementary schools (exclusive of kindergarten) doubled between 1890 and 1960 from 12.5 million to 25.6 million, peaked at 30 million in 1970, dropped to 23.8 million in 1985, and was about 29 million in 2000.

By contrast, the enrollment in four-year tax-supported public high schools doubled from 203,000 in 1890 to 409,000 in 1897, doubled again to 841,000 in 1909, nearly doubled again to slightly over 1.4 million in 1917, doubled again to 3.4 million in 1924, nearly doubled again to 6.6 million in 1940, and doubled again to 14.3 million in 1975. Thanks to the birth dearth of the mid-1970s, enrollment in public high schools in the United States dropped to 11.3 million in 1990, but climbed back up to 13.8 million in 2000 and is expected to set a new record of 14.5 million in 2004.

The population of the United States quadrupled during that one-hundred-year period. Due largely to a decrease in family size, however, elementary school enrollment only doubled, but the enrollment in four-year public high schools increased fifty-five times!

That merits the term "explosive growth"—and explosive growth usually produces unintended consequences!

The number of sixteen-year-olds in the American population nearly tripled from 1.3 million in 1890 to 3.6 million in 1990. The proportion of sixteen-year-olds enrolled in high school in

1890 was less than 4 percent. A century later it was nearly 90 percent.

In the closing years of the nineteenth century, the tax-supported public (common) elementary school had become a widely accepted fact of life in American society. The public high school, however, was still a new creation.

Why?

Why did the enrollment in public high schools suddenly increase so rapidly?

The most obvious reason was the increase in the number of taxpayers who supported the use of public tax funds to finance another layer of public education.

A second reason was the increase in the number of lower-income parents, many of whom were recent immigrants, who came to the United States as the land of hope. Some moved up into that rapidly growing middle class that was one of the remarkable aspects of nineteenth-century America.[1] Many of those lower-income parents who recognized that there was a low ceiling on their own future had powerful upwardly mobile ambitions for their children. They saw education as the way up the social class ladder for their children and the public school as a channel for assimilation into the American culture.

Overlapping that was the growing number of American middle-income parents who began to perceive a high school education for their children as an entitlement, not as a privilege reserved for the children of the wealthy.

Another overlapping force was a product of the Jacksonian revolution of the 1830s. As the American culture evolved from an aristocratic system that reserved higher education for the upper class to a more democratic society, an increasing number of articulate Americans from all social classes argued that education for the masses was an essential foundation stone in a democratic society. That perspective was reinforced by the populist movement. (The other side of that argument was that education for the masses would encourage populism and undermine the aristocratic side of American society. In retrospect, it has turned out that both sides were right!)

A fifth, and extremely influential, factor was simply the disappearance of jobs for youngsters in their middle teens. The first half of the twentieth century brought the transformation of farming. What was a labor intensive occupation in 1900 had become a capital-intensive enterprise by 1950. While the total number of farms increased from 5.7 million in 1900 to 6.8 million in 1935, before plunging to 1.9 million in 1996, the number of big farms increased more dramatically. The number consisting of 500 or more acres tripled from 116,000 in 1890 to 367,000 in 1969. The farm population plummeted from 24.8 million in 1890 to 4.9 million in 1990. The number of hired laborers on the farm plunged from 5.1 million in 1900 to only a million in 1970.

For those who enjoy trivia, a total of 644,000 horse-drawn farm wagons were manufactured in 1904, but only 67,000 in 1921 and 27,000 in 1931. The number of farm tractors grew from 4,000 in 1911 to nearly a million in 1931 to over 3 million in 1949 to 4.8 million in 1966.

A parallel trend occurred in coal mining. The number of coal mining jobs dropped from 723,348 in 1911 to 523,182 in 1933 to 144,480 in 1970 to 100,000 in 1996.

A sixth factor was that this disappearance of jobs in rural America occurred concurrently with a sharp increase in the number of immigrants coming to America. Most of them settled in the cities and were willing to work long hours at low wages. The number of immigrants to these shores increased from 200,000 in 1855 to 405,000 in 1872 to 450,000 in 1900 to over 1 million in 1905 to 1.3 million in 1907 to 1.2 million in 1914—and plummeted to 23,000 in 1933 before going back up to over 100,000 in 1946 for the first time in sixteen years.

That big wave of immigration before World War I increased the demand for places to store the growing number of young teenagers.

A seventh factor was the new child labor laws. During most of the nineteenth century, Massachusetts led the nation in pioneering progressive social legislation; so it is no surprise that the first public high school in the United States was opened in that state in 1821. (That leadership role in progressive state social legislation subsequently was claimed by Wisconsin and more recently by Oregon.) The first state to adopt legislation placing limitations on child labor in factories was Massachusetts in 1836, but it was 1916 before the United States Congress adopted restrictions on child labor.

A progressive view on this subject was articulated in 1907 by an enlightened Massachusetts manufacturer in a speech to the Harvard Teachers Association. He boasted that their progressive state had placed a maximum on the number of hours a fourteen-year-old child could work in a factory at only 58 hours weekly. In his factory, however, he had voluntarily reduced that ceiling to 55 hours![2]

In the late nineteenth century it did appear that the rapid expansion in the number of factories could replace the farms, the forest, and the mines as the place for youngsters in their middle teens to work off most of that abundant supply of energy. But the child labor laws gradually placed a cap on that.

An eighth force to enlarge the role of the public high school came from another direction. This was the growing pressure from professional educators to standardize the public elementary school as an eight-year program. In the nineteenth century, many elementary schools operated with a nine- or ten-grade curriculum. If the elementary school is limited to eight grades, what should be done with those fifteen- and sixteen-year-olds?

The ninth factor was the growing number of states that enacted laws requiring full-time school attendance at least until a child's sixteenth birthday.

Finally, those who argued that public education should be defined as preparation for the twentieth, rather than the twelfth, century began to gain influence. What would be the best place to offer courses in manual training, office skills, and home economics?

On December 3, 1907, President Theodore Roosevelt used

his bully pulpit in his annual message to Congress to declare, "Our school system is gravely defective insofar as it puts a premium upon mere literacy training and tends therefore to train the boy away from the farm and the workshop."[3]

This immediately raised a highly divisive issue that continues to be on the public policy agenda: What is the primary purpose of secondary education? To prepare teenagers for college? To provide a supply of skilled workers for employers? To challenge and enable teenagers to be all that God gave them the gifts to become? To equip them to be contributing and valuable members of a democratic society? Or primarily as a place to warehouse young teenagers until they can enter the labor force?

Filling the Vacuum

While it often is described by the pejorative word compromise, a common response to such a complicated set of questions is, "Yes."

The tax-supported public high school should be able to meet all of those demands. It quickly became apparent that this growing nation needed more high schools.

A minority held out for two sets of public secondary schools. One would be the academic-centered institution. The other would be the trade schools for those who did not want or could not cope with a demanding academic curriculum. Once again the easy answer was "yes" and a "both-and" compromise.

The debate was expanded in 1908 when Harvard President Charles W. Eliot made a speech in Chicago advocating the establishment of trade schools and added the revolutionary suggestion that elementary school teachers should accept responsibility for sorting out students by their "probable destinies" and recommending the appropriate type of secondary education.

Another divisive issue concerned the appropriate education for female teenagers. Should they be equipped to become unpaid homemakers? Or should they be prepared to enter the paid labor force?

The Evolution of the American Public High School

The Emergence of the Big High School

In a provocative book on the changes in the American environment for large institutions, Robert H. Wiebe has pointed out that the last third of the nineteenth century and the first half of the twentieth century provided a hospitable social, economic, and political context for the emergence of very large institutions governed by a highly centralized command and control system.[4] This can be seen in the emergence of large steel corporations, the reduction to three major American-owned motor vehicle companies, the changes in the world of publishing, the mergers that created a few very large Protestant denominations, the expansion of the role of the federal government, the growth of the large research university, and the early near monopoly of three national television networks.

The large public high school should be added to that list. It also should be noted that the last six decades of the twentieth century saw that remarkably supportive national environment for large institutions become increasingly hostile to small institutions.

Back in 1930, the 4.4 million American teenagers enrolled in public high schools were scattered among 23,980 schools for a mean average of 183 students per school. By 1960 that average had climbed to 329. By 1990 the number of four-year public high schools had dropped to 22,000 with a combined enrollment of 11,338 for an average 515 students per school.

By 1994–95 the number of public secondary schools (this figure is from the United States National Center for Education Statistics and includes middle schools) was down to 20,282 and the (mean) average enrollment was 700 students. One-fourth of these schools reported an enrollment of 1,000 or more students, and together they included 56 percent of the total secondary enrollment. Eleven percent of the schools accounted for nearly one-third of the enrollment. At the other end of that size spectrum, one-third of all secondary schools reported an enrollment of fewer than 300 students, but together they accounted for only 6.2 percent of the students. Two-thirds of all students were in schools with an enrollment over 800.

A Century of Explosive Growth

The external national climate in the first several decades of the twentieth century clearly was supportive of this trend toward the creation of large public high schools. It was compatible with the trend toward larger farms, the mergers to produce larger Protestant denominations, larger grocery stores, larger factories, larger medical clinics, and larger universities.

The internal national climate in public education also was supportive of this trend to create large public high schools. State legislatures adopted the policies that provided a financial incentive for small high schools to consolidate. The large high school usually offered a more attractive salary scale for administrators and, sometimes, for teachers.

Another force was the pressure from critics to reach a higher level of efficiency in the administration of tax-supported public high schools. One example was a report submitted to the Chicago Board of Education in 1926 that stated that the current expenses for operating a high school with 2,500 students averaged out to $135.10 per student annually. (The equivalent of approximately $1,300 in current dollars in 2000.) That contrasted with an average cost per student of $123.30 annually in the high school with 4,000 students. A savings of nearly $12 per student could be achieved by expanding the size of the high schools.[5] The report did not identify any of the potential negative consequences for either the teachers or the students of an increase in size.

Back in the last decades of the nineteenth century, the term "school men" often was used to refer to educational leaders. One implication that is more obvious today than it was a century ago is the gender issue. Another is the choice of words emphasized in education. In the 1920s, the term "school executive" began to be used to refer to superintendents and principals. This new title affirmed the heavy administrative responsibilities carried by those in charge. Like the competent business executive of the day, the school executive was expected to acquire the necessary level of expertise required for the "scientific management" of a very large and complex institution called a public school system. This naturally led to an emphasis on efficiency and economy in the management of larger institutions. Ideally the school would be operated like a well-managed business.

The big difference, of course, is that the chief executive officer of a for-profit business is guided by the feedback from the quarterly or monthly profit-and-loss statement. There is one widely accepted and objectively measurable criterion for meaningful self-evaluation.

Unfortunately, in the large public high school, as in a church, there is no single, widely agreed upon, and objectively measurable criterion for meaningful self-evaluation. An attractive substitute was the enrollment. Thus, if bigger is better, then the large school is better than the small school.

The big public high school had become a fact of life, especially in urban and suburban communities, for the socialization of adolescents into American society.

The second half of the twentieth century also brought an operational compromise on the use of tax monies for subsidizing the education of persons attending private schools. While it earned less than universal approval, this compromise included five major components. First, tax-funded educational benefits earned while in military service could be used to attend a private school. Second, the age cohort sentenced by state law to attend school (typically ages 6 to 16) could not receive a tax subsidy to enroll in a private school. That "constitutional limitation," however, could be "outgrown," and when a person enrolled in a private institution of higher education, that restriction was removed. Third, tax funds could be used to subsidize the education of a person, aged 4-18, in a private school if the public schools would not accept that individual because of developmental, physical, emotional, or behavioral limitations. Fourth, if a public school did not exist within a reasonable distance from the student's home, tax monies could be used to subsidize enrollment in a private school. Fifth, and most recently, tax monies could be used to subsidize a child enrolled in a private school if the nearby public school could not provide a satisfactory educational experience for that individual.

Other components of that compromise are still being liti-gated.

The Impact of Research

This increase in the number of very large public high schools took place during a period when a small mountain of research reports and scholarly studies documented the advantages of the small four-year high school with no more than 350 to 500 students. What many scholars endorsed as a landmark study was published in 1964 and summarized much of the research over the previous dozen years. In this book, *Big School, Small School,*[6] the authors focus on the impact of the size of the school on students and contrast the small public high school with the large school.

When they were compared, the authors concluded, students in the small schools (1) participated in a wider variety of extracurricular activities, (2) were much more likely to fill a volunteer position of importance and responsibility, and (3) held these positions of responsibility in a wider variety of activities. They also found that third-year students in the small high schools reported a higher level of satisfaction relating to competence development, to participation in group activities, to being challenged and able to respond to those challenges, and to gaining a sense of belonging and loyalty to that school. They also reported that "marginal" students in the small public high school were less likely to feel alienated from their peers and from the institution than were the marginal students in the large public high schools. Students in the small schools felt more motivated to participate and to accept positions of responsibility and were more likely to express satisfaction in acquiring knowledge and developing intellectual interests. They also expressed a greater zest for living and were less likely to concentrate their academic classes in one discipline.

Two of the key points made in this book were that there is a vast difference between being a spectator and an active participant and that in the small public high school a large proportion of the students are at least at the spectator level of involvement and a far larger proportion are at the active participant level.

One reaction to the book in 1964 was, "That's just common sense! In the large public high school there may be 800 (one-third of the student body) students in the stands watching ten of their schoolmates play a Saturday night basketball game against a rival school. In the small high school there may be 200 students (two-thirds of the student body) watching ten schoolmates in a basketball game."

One major implication is that students who are at least at the spectator level of involvement, and especially those who are at the active participant level, are less likely to feel alienated from their peers and from that school than are the students who are not even at the spectator level of involvement.

Students who are at least at the spectator level of involvement, and especially those who are at the active participant level, are less likely to feel alienated from their peers and from that school than are the students who are not even at the spectator level of involvement.

What was the impact on student behavior of this and hundreds of other research reports on the size of the public high school?[7]

The proportion of public high schools with a thousand or more students doubled from 28 percent in 1970 to 56 percent in 1995. The obvious need was for larger warehouses to store new generations of adolescents.

The warehouse covering ten acres of land provides a far different work environment from the warehouse that covers only an acre or two. The big four-year public high school with more than 1,000 students provides a radically different social setting and learning environment than is found in the four-year high school with 300 or fewer students!

48

A Century of Explosive Growth

Why Build It?

The obvious reason for creating very large public high schools is to house that growing number of students. But that really is a highly superficial explanation. A more comprehensive explanation includes at least a dozen other reasons:

1. A wider range of courses can be offered. One institution can also serve as both a preparatory school and a trade school.

2. The large school can offer more advanced courses for gifted students than the small school can provide.

3. In the large school every teacher can be a specialist. In the small high school one teacher might be required to teach both history and English or both algebra and biology.

4. The large school can provide more jobs for adults. The larger the school, the greater the number of jobs for administrators, coaches, counselors, secretaries, receptionists, bus drivers, coordinators, and safety officers.

5. The high school with a student body of 3,000 will be more effective in serving as a "farm team" for college and university athletic teams than the school with only 350 students.

6. Winning teams in highly competitive interscholastic sports can be useful rallying points for creating a sense of unity in a fragmented urban or suburban community or in an isolated rural community.

7. The large high school can offer students a broader range of choices in extracurricular activities, such as ice hockey, music groups, drama, forensics, and trips to other continents. The guiding generalization is if only one percent of the students are interested, one percent of 300 is too few to offer it, but one percent of 3,000 is sufficient to offer it.

8. While the percentage of students participating in extracurricular activities goes down as enrollment goes up, that is the fault of the students and their parents.

9. The large high school often has a broader geographical service area and, therefore, can bring together a more diverse collection of students. That larger geographical service area also

may provide a larger per-student tax base than is available to the small high school.

10. Most of the students will be bused to the large school, while a larger percentage will walk to a small school serving a small geographical area. While busing adds to the costs, it also enhances safety, provides additional jobs for adults, and reduces the number of students loitering on the campus before and after school.

11. The large school can provide more meaningful challenges that will enable that school to attract more competent administrators. It also will be able to attract teachers with an earned doctorate in an academic discipline such as American history or geography or chemistry or mathematics or English. These exceptionally well-educated teachers will raise the level of the academic offerings.

12. Instead of depending on parents and other volunteers to carry part of the "grunt work" burden, the large school can hire part-time or full-time staff for these duties.

The well-informed and well-intentioned advocates can double or triple the length of that list by adding such advantages as a greater variety of adult role models for the students to emulate, separate parking lots for students and faculty, better access to scholarships for graduating seniors, reduced responsibilities for the volunteer board of education, and the economies of scale that are presumed to be a fringe benefit of big institutions.

The Urge to Merge

One of the normal, natural, and predictable patterns of institutional life in the United States during the twentieth century emerged out of quantitative growth. That quantitative institutional growth creates an urge to merge smaller units with one another. That pattern can be seen in agriculture, in the manufacture and sale of motor vehicles, in banking, in state-sponsored institutions of higher education, in national supermarket chains, in American Protestant Christianity, in the provision of health-care services, in the sale of stocks and bonds, in construction, in the pressures for metropolitan governments, and in scores of other facets of the American economy.

Five of the most common arguments for merging were (1) economy, (2) efficiency, (3) better service to the customer, (4) a reduction in unnecessary "overhead," and (5) the benefits of a larger-scale operation.

Therefore, it should not surprise anyone that this urge to merge became a powerful force in the American public school system. During the middle third of the twentieth century, state legislatures were persuaded to offer financial inducements that would motivate the merger or consolidation of small, locally governed, and tax-supported public schools. The results were dramatic!

The number of locally governed and tax-supported public school districts plummeted from 127,531 in 1932 to fewer than 15,000 in 1998. The number of public schools (all grades) decreased from 274,769 in 1930 to 166,473 in 1950 to under 90,000 in 1998. The biggest decrease, of course, was in the almost complete disappearance of the one-teacher public school. That number plunged from over 200,000 to 1916 to 149,282 in 1930 to 59,652 in 1950 to 35,000 in 1956 to under one thousand today. (If, however, home schooling statistics were included, the total number of one-teacher and two-teacher schools for elementary aged children is now at a record high for the twentieth century and exceeds 300,000).

The number of elementary (grades K–8) school-aged children enrolled in public schools nearly doubled from 18.6 million in 1930 to 36 million in 1998. But the number of public elementary schools decreased by 70 percent from 238,306 to 62,000.

The number of teenagers enrolled in public high schools tripled from 4.4 million in 1930 to 13.5 million in 1998. But the number of public secondary schools decreased from nearly 24,000 in 1930 to 20,000 in 1998.

The usual reasons for consolidation and for the design of very large public high schools cited earlier were offered to support these changes.

The Evolution of the American Public High School

The Law of Unintended Consequences

Every change, however, produces unintended consequences. The creation of the large public high school did achieve many of the goals that were sought. These include a wider range of academic courses available to students, an opportunity for many teachers to specialize in one academic subject and thus spend less time preparing lessons every day, more parking for student-owned motor vehicles, a more attractive environment for students to eat lunch, a higher level of performance in the varsity athletic teams, indoor swimming pools, a full-time school nurse on the premises, better informed career counseling, special classes for gifted students, more generous compensation for staff, tax-supported transportation for a larger proportion of the students, and a much greater variety of extracurricular activities.

Among the unintended consequences, it is easy to identify a baker's dozen:

1. A decrease in parental involvement.

2. A decrease in the sense of "local ownership of our school." The number of locally elected members of the local school board plunged from an estimated 750,000 in 1930 to an estimated 100,000 in 1998, while the total public school enrollment more than doubled. The system of governance moved from participatory democracy to representative democracy to, more recently, interest-group representation.

3. A normal, natural, and predictable consequence of an increase in school size is an increase in the level of anonymity and complexity. Common products of anonymity and complexity are apathy, alienation, adversarial relationships, and anti-social behavior.

4. One of the normal, natural, and predictable patterns in encouraging mergers is to focus on inputs. (In marriage, the slogan was, "Two can live as cheap as one.") The goals of economy and efficiency often are measured in terms of inputs. One consequence is that the new merged institution naturally tends to be concerned about inputs. A school should be primarily concerned with outcomes.

A Century of Explosive Growth

The consolidated public school often is evaluated in terms of inputs, not outcomes. Tax rates, state aid, teachers' compensation, the bus system, safety, schedules, specialized staff positions, the academic credentials of teachers and administrators, a professionally operated cafeteria, profits from vending machines, the opportunities for inservice training for teachers, the availability of a video projector in every classroom, the length of the school year, the increased opportunities for federal grants, and the qualifications of substitute teachers belong on the input side of the ledger. The system becomes the number-one client.

Thus one of the unintended consequences of school consolidation was a reduced emphasis on outcomes and what is happening with and to the students.

5. Perhaps the most subtle unintended consequence is that the proportion of paid educators who are state-certified classroom teachers, but not serving as classroom teachers, keeps going up while the number of classroom teachers who are not certified to teach the subject they are assigned to teach keeps climbing.

6. As mentioned elsewhere, the larger the school, the more likely the daily schedule will be dictated by the school bus system.

7. While no one can prove cause and effect, the larger the school, the greater the proportion of students who are tardy or absent.

8. While no one can prove cause and effect, the record is clear. The larger the public school system, the greater the proportion of parents who choose the home schooling system.

9. While a product of many factors, the larger the school system, the more attractive is the option for experienced classroom teachers to elect early retirement.

10. While this may have been an intended, but rarely articulated, consequence, one result is the larger the school system, the smaller the proportion of paid staff who are classroom teachers and the larger the proportion who are bus drivers, nurses, principals, safety officers, secretaries, administrators, and other specialists.

11. While exceptions do exist, the basic generalization is that the larger the enrollment of a public school, the higher the per-student annual operating expenditures will be.

> **From the students' perspective, the most serious unintended consequence of the large public high school was to produce an ecological environment that is incompatible with, and at times even hostile to, the creation of effective learning communities.**

12. The larger the school system, the greater the felt need to satisfy distant bureaucratic agencies (state government, accrediting agencies, federal agencies, etc.), rather than to create effective learning environments.

13. Since thirteen is widely perceived to be an unlucky number, the most serious unintended consequence of the urge to merge to produce large public high schools is placed last. This is the central theme of this book and is discussed in more detail in the next chapter.

From the students' perspective, the most serious unintended consequence of the large public high school was to produce an ecological environment that is incompatible with, and at times even hostile to, the creation of effective learning communities. (This is the subject of the last chapter.)

Chapter Three

THE FACTORY MODEL[1]

T
he first seven decades of the twentieth century brought an explosive growth in the enrollment of public high schools. It also brought the large corporate farm, the large sports stadium, the large public university, the large airport terminal, the large retail shopping mall, the large research hospital, the large multisite automobile company, the large Protestant megachurch, the large public-housing project, and the large military base.

This context, plus the "big business" orientation of the American economy, provided a supportive context for encouraging the emergence of the large public high school. That cultural environment plus the rapid increase in enrollments plus the concept of "economy of scale" plus the widespread acceptance of a value system that declared "bigger is better" supported the creation of public four-year high schools with an enrollment in the 800 to 5,000 range.

From the professional educator's perspective, a logical consequence was a need for superior administrators. An increasing number of universities began to offer a doctorate in educational administration. From a teacher's perspective, the large public high school also offered more opportunities for specialization.

From a student's perspective, the large public high school required a new metaphor. For a small percentage a useful analogy was the university. High school could be conceptualized as a mini-university. Some students referred to a respected teacher as "Prof." Several high schools created a staff position for the

"Dean of Students." An increasing number offered advanced placement courses taught at the college level. The most gifted science students could be challenged to undertake research projects that were on a university level of sophistication.

The Second Place

From other students' perspectives, however, the more realistic model was the factory. Their father got up in the morning, ate breakfast, walked or took a bus or drove to work. The workplace often was housed in a big building and was administered by a number of trained adults. For the most part the work was repetitive, dull, and boring, and it rarely challenged the workers' creativity.

The big break in the routine of the day was at lunch when the workers had a brief time in a controlled environment to socialize with one another. Those who functioned within a short time frame spent the afternoon looking forward to quitting time. The older workers with a longer time frame looked forward to their upcoming vacation or to their retirement.

After work, many stopped at the third place in their lives, a bar, to "hoist a few with the boys." Their home was the first place in their lives. There they were known by their family members and relatives as husband, father, breadwinner, disciplinarian, grandfather, and, possibly, a "soft touch." The factory was the second place in their lives. There they were known by their peers for what they did, for their skill with their hands. The tavern on the way home was a place where they were known by their friends for who they were as a person, not by what they did for a living or by their kinfolk.[2] That second place was organized around tasks, titles, marketable work skills, a time clock, and functions. The third place was organized around fellowship, social skills, friendships, refreshments, banter, and community.

As the decades of the twentieth century rolled by, the owners and managers in the best of the factories began to realize that one expression of enlightened self-interest would be to attempt to transform the workplace into an attractive third place. One way to do that would be to organize employer-sponsored bowling teams and softball teams, to schedule an annual company picnic for workers and their families, to give highly publicized awards to workers or teams of workers for outstanding performance, to publish a company newsletter given free to every worker, and, perhaps, even to have someone compose a company song to be sung at special occasions. Jackets, caps, and golf shirts inscribed with the company insignia were given to workers on the anniversary of the beginning of their employment or for membership on a company sports team.

Several years ago a student in a large public high school described his life in these terms: "My dad gets up in the morning, eats breakfast, and rides to work in a company-owned van. He has to show his I.D. badge to be admitted into the building where he works. He spends the morning engaged in dull, boring routine and repetitive work on an assembly line that moves past him at a company-determined pace. He enjoys his lunch break, goes back to work, looks forward to quitting time, and eventually finishes work for the day. After work, he walks a few hundred feet to a bar where he spends an hour or so with his friends and catches a ride home with one of them. He plays shortstop on the company softball team, so in cool weather he wears a jacket the company gave him with the team logo on the front and the company name on the back. He also has three or four golf shirts with the company insignia on them. If you ask him for the birthdates of his three kids, he has to stop and think; but he can tell you immediately how many days he has left to work before he can retire."

"That's interesting," I commented, "but I asked you to describe your typical day at school."

"I get up in the morning, eat breakfast, and catch a school-owned bus to school," he replied. "I have to show my I.D. card to get into the building. I spend the morning trying to open my mind to catch the information the teachers want to drop in there. Unlike my dad's assembly line, where he stays in one place all morning, I move from room to room on a schedule set by the school administrators. At lunch I enjoy socializing with my friends at the same table every day in the cafeteria. After lunch I go to another set of dull, boring assembly line assignments and check my watch frequently to see how long before the last bell will ring. Most of the year I go from school to the mall to hang out with friends for an hour or two. In the spring we have baseball practice after school, and last year I earned my letter jacket, which has the name of the school on the back and our team's insignia on the front. Since I don't have a car, I have to catch a ride home with a friend from the mall or from baseball practice. My dad and I get home about the same time every evening. I don't always remember the birthdays of my parents, my brother, and my sister, but you can ask me anytime and I can tell you exactly how many days until I graduate and can go out on my own."

"Are you telling me you and your dad lead parallel lives?" I asked.

"Yes and no," he replied. "Yes, we both have dull, boring day jobs. We both are looking forward to when we can get out of there, and we both find the best part of the day is when we can hang out with our friends. No, one big difference is he gets paid for that day job, and I don't."

This student failed to identify a second big difference. The factory where his dad works is organized around two compatible goals. One is to assemble high-quality automobiles. The other is to generate profits for the corporation and stockholders. The intellectual and social improvement of the workers is far lower on that list of company goals.

By contrast, some people believe the primary purpose of a public high school should be focused on the intellectual, social, moral, ethical, and physical development of teenagers. In that factory, the focus is on the assembly of automobiles. That institution called the large high school has many constituents. Who is number one?

What Is the Dividing Line?

From this observer's perspective, the most significant line of demarcation dividing the public high school student body into subgroups is not age and grade. The most useful dividing line, if the goal is to create effective learning communities, is between the students who perceive the school to be the second place in their daily lives and those who look forward every morning to a school that represents third place in their lives.

Should the ideal public high school be perceived by students as the second place in their lives where they are known as freshmen, sophomores, juniors, and seniors and by the classes they take? Or should the ideal public high school be perceived as the third place in their lives where they are known and affirmed for who they are as individuals, where their distinctive gifts and skills are given an outlet, where they find a sense of community, and where their social skills are enhanced?

For many teenagers, that third place is found in competitive interscholastic athletics, as a member of the band, as a reporter or editor of the school newspaper, as a member of a drama or vocal group, or in some other extracurricular activity. Is it possible for a classroom experience to be that place?

The answer, of course, is yes! One example is the well-designed seminar for doctoral students in the research university.

The typical public high school classroom, however, rarely will serve as that third place for more than a few students unless it is organized like a good third place, rather than like a college classroom.

One Criterion for Evaluation

Many of today's high school students, especially the juniors and seniors, hold part-time jobs during the school year. When the group includes several persons who are employed outside the home or in a parent's business during the school year, I ask that group the either-or question described in chapter 1: "All of us feel a need for feedback on how we're doing. One example of feedback is a report card. Another is our paycheck. For those of you who are employed during the school year, which do you find to be the more meaningful expression of feedback on how you're doing? Your report card or your paycheck?"

Typically 5 to 30 percent raise their hands when I ask, "Report card?" The vast majority, however, usually raise their hands when I ask, "Paycheck?"

Among the spontaneous explanations I hear are, "My parents think it should be my report card, but they're more impressed with how much money I bring home!" "Hardly anyone pays any attention to report cards anymore."

In one group an argument broke out immediately after I polled the students on that either-or question. They could not agree on whether their high school report cards were issued once, twice, or three times each semester.

Many factory workers also see their paychecks as a source of feedback on how they are doing.

Who Goes to Your High School?

One of the questions I have asked teenagers for many years is, "Who goes to your high school?" Since these conversations are carried out in two languages—theirs and mine—occasionally we need to translate terms and concepts not familiar to the other side. I begin by explaining that I am interested in discovering the labels applied in their high school to the various tribes or social networks that constitute the student body. Under the broad umbrella of social networks are concepts identified in their language as cliques, groups, gangs, clubs, teams, and friendship circles.

Not once in over two thousand responses has a teenager referred to the categories labeled freshmen, sophomores, juniors, and seniors. The most frequently voiced labels include "jocks," "chimneys," "druggies," "goths," "bandos," "nerds," "stoners," "trendies," "skaters," "hip hops," "preppies," (which may refer to a dress code or to students who are preparing an impressive dossier in hopes of being admitted to the college or university of their choice), "Cubans," "cheerleaders," "rednecks," "blacks," "freaks," "ravers," "straights," "techies," and "rebels."

Many years ago I heard the term "student" for the first time. I had assumed that all of these youngsters were students, so I had to ask for a translation. The explanation was this: "Those are the kids who come to class and are practically invisible. Either they don't have any friends or they have only the one friend who is another student." More recently a tall, handsome, blond-haired seventeen-year-old male added "Parallel Parkers" to the list. Once again I had to confess my ignorance and ask for a translation. "Those are the kids who sleep around" was the reply. I was the only person in the room who blinked.

Most of the high school students I meet are either members of one or more social networks or find their need to be accepted as a member of a peer group fulfilled in a church youth group. A disproportionately large number of the male students also make it clear to me that school is the second place in their lives, not third. Therefore, their worldview should not be assumed to represent the perspective of all other students.

When I suggest that the distinction between a second place and a good third place is the most useful line of demarcation in categorizing high school students, the majority insist that is not true for their school. They contend that the key dividing line is between those students who are members of one or more social networks in that school and those who find that their most valuable social network exists outside the school or who are loners without membership in any social network.

This often evokes a "What's the difference?" response from one or two who have followed that part of our conversation most closely.

Chapter Four

DOES THE ENVIRONMENT MATTER?

eople teach, but the institutions which people build also teach."[1]

It is the last half of the ninth inning on a Friday night, and the home team, the Boston Red Sox, are trailing the hated New York Yankees by three runs. The first batter grounds out to the shortstop. The second strikes out. The third singles. The fourth also singles. The fifth walks. The bases are loaded! The next batter takes the count to three balls and two strikes, fouls off the next two pitches, and then hits a home run. The home team wins! The fans are wild with excitement.

On the following Saturday afternoon four of the Red Sox fans who attended the game meet together to attend the memorial service for a mutual friend who died three days earlier in a tragic automobile accident. The memorial service is held in a church none of the four had ever entered previously. A eulogy by the brother of the deceased recaptures the spirit and special gifts of that man and evokes several chuckles and bits of subdued laughter. Except for that break, it is a solemn and sorrowful forty-minute experience. The four friends leave together and do not speak to one another until they get in their car to drive away.

The night before, they, along with most of the fans in Fenway Park, stood to watch as the last four batters came to the plate. When it was clear that the long fly ball was going to land in the seats, they screamed with joy, clapped one another on the back, shook hands with total strangers, and acted as if they had just won the lottery.

Does the Environment Matter?

The environment in the ballpark not only approved that kind of behavior, but also elicited that kind of excited behavior. Fourteen hours later, the environment in the church filled with nearly three hundred mourners evoked a radically different kind of behavior from these four men.

Which Side of the Counter?

It is eleven thirty on a Tuesday morning on Main Street. The first customer of the day walks into a small retail store that sells men's suits. The customer, who believes shopping for a new suit is only more fun than going to the dentist for a root canal, is delighted to find an off-the-rack suit that fits perfectly, is exactly the right color and fabric, and is priced sixty dollars below what he expected to pay. The proprietor throws in a necktie as a gesture of goodwill.

That evening the customer shows his new suit to his wife when she gets home from work. She compliments him on his taste and luck. They agree, "This was a great day!"

The proprietor goes home that evening and tells his wife, "I should have sold the store last fall when that fellow came by who wanted to buy it! Yesterday I had four customers all day, one bought a suit, one bought a shirt and necktie, one bought four pairs of socks, and the other didn't buy a thing. Today I had only three customers. This morning one person bought a suit I've had on sale for seven months and have marked down twice. So I only made ten dollars on that deal. One came in at noon, looked around for a half hour and left without buying a thing. The third came in about two o'clock and bought a shirt. I've had it! The malls have killed my business."

Two people participate in the same experience. One describes it as delightful. The other views it as one more step on the downhill road to economic oblivion.

What Is Your Perspective?

The readers of this book will bring a variety of perspectives that will influence their reaction to the contents. That list of

63

readers conceivably could include parents, professional educators, taxpayers, school board members, law enforcement officials, counselors, stepparents, college and university teachers, preachers, elected governmental leaders, journalists, nurses, architects, editors, grandparents, high school graduates of the 1980s and 1990s, athletic coaches, and a few of today's high school students.

Each one will bring a personal perspective and his or her own value system. Nearly all will also bring (1) a diagnosis of what is wrong with today's public high schools, (2) a diagnosis of what is wrong with today's teenagers, and (3) a prescription for both of those problems.

This observer brings a different perspective, which includes two questions. First, does the analogy of the large public high school resembling a prison reflect contemporary reality? Second, who is in the best position to answer the first question? This book is based on the assumption that the people in the best position to answer that question are the students enrolled in today's large public schools.[2]

A third question fits into the "So what?" category. What difference does it make how the students view their high school? The answer to that question is the theme of this chapter and is one of the foundational assumptions on which this book rests. It begins with the admonition that every system produces what that system is designed to produce. To change the language, the environment tells people how to behave. An exciting baseball game tells people it is okay to engage in a certain type of behavior.

The environment tells people how to behave.

The solemn atmosphere of that memorial service told those four men not to dress the same they had the night before and to behave in a more subdued manner. The length and the slow pace of the line of mourners wishing to express their condolences to the family told them their schedule did not permit that courtesy.

The environment can communicate messages to those who are not present or have not been there before.

Why do high school students behave the way they do?

In other words, why do high school students behave the way they do? There are many variables and influences, but at the top of that list is the environment—the cultural, physical, pedagogical, and social atmosphere of a particular school. The most obvious illustration of this is that the behavior patterns of students in a four-year high school with a total enrollment of 150 and six teachers is vastly different from the behavior patterns of those enrolled in a high school with 3,500 students and 350 teachers, counselors, administrators, bus drivers, safety officers, cafeteria workers, and other paid staff.

All of us behave differently if we are in a room with 150 people, all of whom are friends and acquaintances, than when we are in a setting with 3,500 people, nearly all of whom are strangers.

This is not a revolutionary new idea! For thousands of years military leaders have recognized that their troops can be organized in a manner that will encourage many to flee when the enemy approaches. A different formation, however, will motivate most of those same troops to be willing to die for their comrades.

In recent years, three terms have been invented to describe this concept. One is "Ecological Psychology." Another is "Ecological Environment."[3] A simpler one is "Setting."[4] The pioneers in this field, as well as contemporary researchers, agree that the environment influences human behavior. A simple example is the choice of clothing of the person going for a two-mile outdoor walk in Montana in January and at the same time a person going for a two-mile outdoor walk in south

Florida. The social and physical environment plus the people are crucial elements of the conceptual framework for this worldview, but so are such influences as local customs, institutional traditions, laws, language, money, and scores of other cultural variables.

Most of the proposed reforms of public education in America in recent years have included changing the setting for learning.

From this observer's perspective, however, the beginning point should not be on proposed changes in the ecological environment or the setting for secondary education, but rather on reaching agreement on two other issues. The first is agreement that the setting does influence the behavior of high school students. The second is agreement that the students' perception of that setting is the most important issue. Students react to their perception of reality, not to someone else's perception. Parents, for example, may perceive that participation in certain "extreme" sports is somewhere between dangerous and suicidal. The sixteen-year-old, however, may perceive that sport as challenging and participation in it as thrilling. Likewise, police officers may perceive an automobile speed of 80 miles an hour on a residential street to be dangerous, but the seventeen-year-old male, who perceives himself to be immortal, agrees that is a dangerous speed only if someone else is driving.

This is not to suggest that the perceptions of the parents or teachers or administrators of that high school environment are unimportant. They are very important! Those adults also react to their perceptions of reality. One central point of this book, however, is that the students react to their perceptions—and they may conclude that the perceptions of parents, teachers, and administrators are uninformed, unrealistic, biased, obsolete, irrelevant, and perhaps even counterproductive.

Those students who perceive their high school environment to resemble the environment of a prison naturally will tend to behave like prisoners. That does not mean, however, that because they perceive the principal to be the warden, the principal automatically will identify with and accept the role of warden!

Does the Environment Matter?

Our Blaming Culture

A fourth question, which everyone is quick to answer, is, "When something goes tragically wrong, who is to blame?"

The disaster at Columbine High School demonstrated how easy it is in our culture to answer that question. The answers included parents, teachers, school administrators, television, gun dealers, today's teenagers, motion pictures, our affluent society, law enforcement officials, counselors, athletes, video games, the growing societal affirmation of violence as a way to settle disputes, politicians, the churches, an excessively permissive social system, and an inadequate number of safety officers in the school.

At the top of the list should be the ecological environment of the large public high school.

A fifth question concerns the role of today's high school students in this facet of American life. That question also has many answers, but for the majority of the students the number-one role is to serve as the chief victim of a system that produces what that system is designed to produce. If the system is designed to create boring experiences in the classroom, then the majority of students will be bored. This, of course, opens the door for people to play one of the most enjoyable games in American culture, called "Blaming the Victim."

Finally, we come to the question of what motivated a grandfather to write this book.

A bulk mail promotional piece for a magazine arrived recently in our mailbox. The opening sentence of the cover was, "Are sports, television, and the movies all we have left in common?"

My immediate response was, "I hope not! First on that list should be to make this a better world for children."

One way to do that would be to enlist parents, educators, religious leaders, radio, television, newspapers, elected governmental officials, journalists, and others in a crusade to help make this a better world for children.

Theoretically the best place to begin is with couples who are expecting their first child. The second best place to begin is with the parents of babies and very young children.[5] The third best place is to focus on children ages four to ten or twelve years and their parents. The fourth best place is with middle-school children. The fifth best point of intervention is with the large public school, and that often includes a heavy burden of remedial action.

If, however, that is only the fifth best point of intervention, why not begin at an earlier stage of a child's life?

Five reasons can be offered here. First, concurrently the pain and the discontent are greatest in the large public high school. Second, it is easier and quicker to design an intervention strategy for 10,000 institutions than for one directed at a hundred million parents, children, educators, and public officials. Third, it is easier to change an institutional culture than to change the value systems, habits, convictions, and lifestyles of individuals. The big difference is if the culture of an institution cannot be changed, it can be replaced. This already is happening with charter schools, the stock market, the locally owned telephone system, and the delivery and financing of health-care services.

Fourth, and most important, a growing cadre of potential allies already is at work in transforming the environment of several large public high schools. Mine is **not** a lone voice crying in the wilderness.

Finally, it would be ethically wrong to respond to the pleas for help of today's high school students with the comment, "You were born too soon for us to be able to help you."

What Does the Environment Tell Us?

In December 1941 and all of 1942 the national environment in the United States urged eighteen- and nineteen-year-old males (the draft began with twenty-year-olds until early 1943) to enlist in military service. A couple of million of us, many in our first year or two of college or the university, did that.

Twenty-five years later the national environment had changed. The message received by millions of young men was, "If you want to celebrate your twenty-fifth birthday, don't go to Vietnam!"

Does the Environment Matter?

For many decades the high school environment told teenage girls, "You have two choices. You can take the short road and prepare to become a wife and mother, or you can choose a longer route and be a secretary, a clerk, a teacher, a telephone operator, a domestic servant, a nurse, or a typist before you become a wife and mother."

It may take time, but it is possible to change the messages a high school sends to the students![6]

Television, law enforcement, major league sports, and their peers tell young American-born black males, "You have four roads to wealth open to you—professional basketball, professional football, professional baseball, and crime. Take your pick!" Professional baseball is now coming in fourth in that array of choices.

For three hundred years the American culture told boys, "First, your best opportunity for your future is to follow the same occupation, trade, or profession your father chose. Second, choose a wife from among the women who live within thirty miles of where you live." World War II made both of those admonitions obsolete.

The modern prison tells the newly arrived inmate, "Join a gang or expect trouble." The large public school tells the first-year student who just moved in from out of town, "Find a clique you're comfortable with or look forward to four lonely years here."

The small public high school sends a message to the student with a slightly above-average level of athletic ability, "Pick the sport(s) of your choice. If you don't make the starting lineup, you almost certainly will end up on the squad."

The message received by the student with a slightly above-average level of athletic ability in the very large high school is, "Don't bother even coming out for this sport. You almost certainly won't make the team, and you will end up with one more message of rejection."

The junior or senior in the 350-student high school probably has one chance in 150 of being elected president of the student body. The junior or senior in the public high school with an enrollment of 3,500 may have one chance in 1,500 of being elected president of the student body.

While many of the professionals declared that the primary purpose of the public high school in the closing years of the nineteenth century was to prepare students for life in a democratic society, that did not necessarily coincide with the image perceived by the student.

What Was the Model?

The pioneers who created that rapidly growing number of public high schools in the late nineteenth and early twentieth centuries were faced with a fundamental question: What is a public high school? In the northeastern states, the answer was simple. A tax-supported high school should resemble the privately financed college preparatory school or the private academy, but be open to all social strata.[7]

In the rest of the nation an alternative model was the tax-supported, locally controlled, and evangelical (or pietistic) Protestant public elementary school. In addition to teaching rudimentary skills in reading, writing, and arithmetic, the typical public elementary school of the nineteenth century also sought to transmit to children a basic Protestant moral value, a Christian standard of ethical behavior, and a patriotic spirit.

In a delightful recent essay, Elliott A. Wright suggests that the changing religious theme in the common schools reflected the trend in nineteenth-century America as it evolved from a "stern Calvinism . . . to a mellow Methodism."[8]

The good public high school of 1935 would retain age as the basic line of demarcation for dividing the student body into groups, be staffed with somewhat better educated teachers, be locally controlled, and transmit the community value system to the students.

A third source for an answer was to ask the professional educators. While they differed sharply on many details and were divided over whether the primary purpose should be preparation for college or preparation for life, most agreed that the school should be organized around teaching the subjects the teachers liked to teach and were academically trained to teach. They proposed the institutional environment should be designed to resemble a college rather than the pietistic Protestant public elementary school of the day. The daily schedule would be primarily organized around the teaching of academic subjects, not around the transmission of virtues, patriotism, cooperation, democratic ideals, or an evangelical Protestant religion. In the South, of course, there was a greater emphasis on the transmission to students of the core of the Christian faith, of the superiority of the white race, and of social-class distinctions.

A Fourth Answer

While it was rarely articulated this bluntly, a fourth reason to organize tax-supported public schools was to answer that pressing question, "What do we do with the kids who have graduated from elementary school and are too young to enter an already crowded labor force?"

One earlier answer was to put them to work on the farm, in the mines, or in the forests. That alternative was beginning to become an obsolete solution, as was pointed out in the chapter 2. Another answer had been to keep them in elementary school for an extra year or two. But that created huge problems for the teachers with six-year-olds and sixteen-year-olds in the same classroom.

The attractive solution was to warehouse these adolescents for a year or two or more in the public high school.

A Good Warehouse

Among the characteristics of a good warehouse are these: (1) The contents are protected from the weather. (2) It is a safe place, and the contents are protected from harm. (3) A high value is placed on order. (4) The person in charge possesses a reasonable degree of competence in managing a warehouse but does not need to display the characteristics of an effective leader. (5) The costs, both capital and operating, are within the capacity of the consumers to pay. (6) Space always is available for additional inventory to be stored. (7) It will not be a blight on the landscape and may even be a source of pride to the nearby residents. (8) It does not bar customers on the basis of race, religion, social class, or gender (that last line of demarcation is still being debated). (9) The staff of the warehouse will be able to maintain control and will never have to request intervention by the local police department. (10) In today's world all newly arrived merchandise to be stored may have to be examined or passed through a metal detector. (11) When a customer comes to withdraw what had been stored, it will be at least in as good condition as when it had been admitted earlier. And (12) it will meet or exceed current standards for such buildings.

The Criteria for Evaluation

A well-run warehouse is an economical and efficient operation. How does one measure efficiency? A carefully thought-out response to that question was prepared by the adults responsible for operating one of the larger warehouse systems in the United States during the first decades of the twentieth century. It quickly was copied and utilized by the managers of other warehouses.

The chief designer for this system of evaluation was William A. Wirt while he was superintendent of schools in Bluffton, Indiana. In 1908 he was hired to be the superintendent of schools in Gary, Indiana, and there he perfected the design. He came to a school system in which nearly all of the classrooms were unoccupied for 120 or more hours out of 168 hours in the average week during the school year. This meant the efficiency level of the operation was below 25 percent!

Wirt brought his "Gary Platoon Plan" with him from Bluffton and reorganized the Gary school system. This called for "platoons" of students to move from room to room on a regular schedule. The typical student's schedule called for two ninety-minute periods, each spent studying a basic subject.

Does the Environment Matter?

That was supplemented by six thirty-minute blocks of time in special subjects, such as music or shop. That six-hour day was interrupted by sixty to seventy-five minutes for lunch. The students moved from room to room, and every room was in use for at least six hours daily. In addition, the "Gary Plan" subsequently was expanded to include evening and Saturday classes. By beginning earlier in the day, running late in the evening, and scheduling Saturday uses, several superintendents were able to move their efficiency rating from 15 to 20 percent in the typical school week up to 40 percent!

A man by the name of John Franklin Bobbit eventually became the self-appointed, number-one national advocate of this "Work-Study-Play" adaptation of scientific management to the large public high school.[9]

The impact of moving from one room to another on (1) peer relationships among the students, (2) creating and nurturing a positive learning environment, (3) the continuity of the learning process, and (4) teacher/student relationships was largely ignored. The driving criterion for self-evaluation was to increase the use of the physical facilities. A well-managed warehouse places a premium on maximizing use of the building!

From the perspective of the ecological environment, this criterion for the evaluation of an efficient public high school raises some interesting issues.

Back in the early years of the twentieth century, it was not unusual for the first-year students in the four-year public high school to include a substantial number of recent graduates of one-teacher, eight-grade elementary schools. These schools devoted eight years to teaching impressionable children, typically ages six to fourteen, that a positive learning environment includes (1) meeting in the same educational setting all day, week after week and year after year; (2) relating to the same adult teacher all day, week after week and usually for a minimum of three to four consecutive years; (3) relating to a peer group that typically would have a turnover of only 15 percent, more or less, annually; (4) working with one teacher who is competent to teach a variety of subjects at six to eight different grade levels; (5) learning in an environment that not only made it easy for older children to teach younger children, but also frequently made that a requirement on the playground as well as in the classroom; (6) creating a wide variety of easy opportunities for participants to meet and make new friends; (7) placing a low ceiling on the number of people in that ecological environment so everyone could easily and quickly learn the name of everyone else in that setting; (8) providing a setting that makes it relatively easy to enter into long-term relationships with peers; (9) making cooperation a norm if we expect to be able to live and learn together all day, week after week for several years; and (10) challenging nearly every child to be both a learner and a teacher on many different occasions in the classroom or on the playground during those eight years together.

Eventually many of the fourteen-year-old graduates of that learning environment enrolled in a nearby four-year public high school organized on the Gary Platoon Plan. This design called for students to change rooms six to nine times daily, to meet a new adult in each room, and, frequently, to relate to a new mix of peers several times every day. One peer group might lose 10 to 80 percent of its members every time the bell rang.

From a teacher's perspective that often meant getting acquainted with 150 to 180 or more students every year, which contrasted with the one-teacher elementary school where the beginning of the second year of the teacher's tenure required getting acquainted with three to twelve new pupils every fall.

What was the response of the fourteen-year-old who left that one-teacher school with thirty or so pupils after eight years to enroll in a public high school organized on the platoon plan? A natural, normal, and predictable response would be, "I don't know what's going on around here, but this certainly is not a positive learning environment. To me, it resembles a large warehouse run by and for the convenience of adults who need a place to store kids like me."

As we enter the new millennium, and as we benefit from four decades of research and insights on the influence of the environment on human behavior, it is easy to dismiss the Gary Plan's emphasis on efficiency and economy as ancient history. While many readers may find this difficult to believe, it is relatively easy today to find a public high school that is designed on the assumption that (1) a competent teacher can relate effectively to 150 new students every year; (2) the learning environment is enhanced when the students move to a different room every 45 to 50 minutes and the composition of the peer group changes every 45 to 50 minutes; (3) today's teenagers are comfortable in a learning setting in which many of the participants are strangers and some are only acquaintances; (4) the cell phone now enables friends to engage in oral communication with friends in other parts of the building, so being with the same social network in the same room all day is less important than it once was; (5) if a person can relate effectively to 25-35 people in a group, he or she should be able to relate effectively to a new group in a new physical setting every hour; (6) the important point of continuity in learning is in the joy of learning, not in the continuity of the ecological or learning environment; (7) the student's capability to learn will be enhanced by being exposed to several different teachers during the course of one day; (8) the school should be organized on the principle that adults are the teachers and students are the learners; (9) what is called cooperation in some places is identified as cheating in high school; (10) order is a high priority in operating an efficient warehouse, an efficient factory, an efficient prison, or an efficient public high school; (11) security is a high priority in operating a warehouse, a factory, a prison, or a public school; (12) students should expect that their learning environment will be determined not by what they experienced in elementary school, but by what they may experience if and when they go on to college or to a university; and (13) anonymity, alienation, and complexity are valuable components of an effective learning environment.

The Power of Evaluation

In the ideal world we measure what is important. In the real world of long-established big institutions, what we measure becomes important.[10] A simple and highly visible example of that generalization is the reliance on average expenditures per student to evaluate public school systems. Public schools were not created to collect and spend money. They were created to educate children, to transmit the culture and values of that community to the next generation, and to supplement the efforts of kinfolk in the rearing of children. It is difficult to design objective criteria for evaluating the success of a school in achieving any one of those goals. It is relatively easy, however, to divide total operating expenses by the number of students and arrive at an average figure. That is close to an objective number and has become a widely used criterion in comparing one school system with another. The only serious debate is over whether a small number is better than a big number (the standard up through the 1930s) or a big number is superior to a small number (the standard for the past several decades). In an economically depressed era, the smaller number is good. In an economically affluent era, the bigger number is better.

Public schools were not created to collect and spend money. They were created to educate children, to transmit the culture and values of that community to the next generation, and to supplement the efforts of kinfolk in the rearing of children.

That was the number-one flaw in the design of the Gary Platoon Plan. It called for measuring the utilization of rooms as a criterion for evaluation. That made room utilization important. Since it was difficult to agree on equally objective criteria for measuring what happened to the quality of the learning environment or to the progress of the students in learning or in being socialized into the local culture, what was measured moved to the top of the scale in the evaluation process.

Does the Environment Matter?

The Importance of Place

A second big flaw in the Gary Platoon Plan was that it ran counter to one of the central dynamics of human behavior. This is the importance of place and the value of place as a point of continuity in life.[11]

One of the most significant and widely overlooked differences between the eight-grade, one-room elementary school of the 1930s and the contemporary large public high school is the loss of "my place." In that one-room school, every student had a personal space that included a seat and a desk. That place might be selected by the student, or it could have been assigned by the teacher. In that school everyone knew, "This is Dan's desk, and that is Mary's desk." That desk also was a place a pupil could store a limited amount of personal property.

The Gary Platoon Plan wiped out the possbility of each student's having "my own place." As the students moved from one classroom to another, the cult of efficiency demanded that they surrender that luxury of "my own place." Eventually the locker in the corridor became a depository for one's personal possessions, but it was far from an adequate substitute for "my desk." In some high schools, the teacher also had to surrender the comfort of "my room and my desk" to share space in the teachers' lounge.

When adults are forced to evacuate their homes because of the threat of a forest fire or a hurricane, one normal and predictable consequences is a high level of stress. Many generations ago colleges recognized that leaving home to go to a residential school was a stress-producing experience for eighteen-year-olds. To compensate for that, the colleges constructed dormitories. The typical first-year student arrives in late summer. The first act on arrival is not to visit classrooms, but rather to go directly to "my dorm" to see "my room" and to meet "my future roommate."

One characteristic of a dysfunctional organization is a failure to recognize and affirm the importance of place in the daily life of normal human beings.

The Evolution of the American Public High School

* * * * *

The ethnic Albanians who returned to Kosovo in mid-1999 after weeks of being refugees were not surprised, but they were dismayed to discover the place to which they were returning was not the same as the place they had left.

* * * * *

The graduate of a public school in the class of 1990 returns, for the first time, a decade later and reflects, "This place sure has changed since I left."

* * * * *

In 1741 James Boswell wrote, "I have often amused myself with thinking how different the same place is to different people."[12]

* * * * *

Mayors recognize and affirm the fact that a city is not simply a unit of local government. Instead, it is a collection of places.

* * * * *

One of the reasons why urban renewal projects were so widely opposed is because, by definition, they were a threat to the continuity in life that people find in place.

* * * * *

The old rural one-teacher, eight-grade elementary school was perceived by most pupils as one place. The modern public high school is a collection of places. The football stadium may come the closest of any one physical setting to being perceived as a common place by large numbers of people.[13]

An individual's sense of belonging often is expressed by the choice of pronouns. That one-room elementary school taught most of the pupils, This is "our school" or "my school." The children were expected to share in the work of keeping the building and the grounds clean. The older children took turns at the outdoor pump to provide the water for the indoor drinking fountain and for the washbasin. They worked industriously to clean that one room before the parents' visit. The teacher was the supervisor, but the children were part of the work force required to maintain "our school."

In the most sophisticated eight- or nine-room elementary school, the paid custodian performed most of the maintenance and the pupils referred to that space as "Mrs. Jones's room," which was across the hall from "Mr. Smith's classroom." The message that the students carried a responsibility for the care of "our classroom" was diluted as the perception of ownership was transferred to adults.

In the large public high school in which both the teachers and the students migrate from room to room during the day, a different message is received by the students. This is "their" building, and "they" have the responsibility to maintain it. One way to even the score for a perceived wrong is to "trash their building." A more radical way to even the score is to trash the enemy.

The sense of ownership of physical space can either teach good citizenship or raise the level of alienation.

* * * * *

The movement of the capital of the reunited Germany from Bonn to Berlin required the expenditure of billions of German deutsche marks—but the symbolic importance of place justified that expenditure.

Should the capital of Israel be located in Tel Aviv or in Jerusalem? That is a quarrel over the symbolic importance of place.

* * * * *

How could students be encouraged to return to Columbine High School in Littleton in the late summer of 1999 with a minimum degree of fear? One part of the answer was to repair all the damage to the structure so that place would appear to be undamaged and safe.

* * * * *

Married couples who sleep in the same bed usually find it more comfortable if she is on her side and he is on his side of the bed.

The Evolution of the American Public High School

* * * * *

While there may be a dozen supermarkets within a short driving distance, most suburbanites prefer to buy their groceries at the same one or two or three places week after week.

* * * * *

Many years ago, Don and Mary Johnson, a couple with five children, moved into a new house with four bedrooms on the second floor. The largest, with its own private bath, was occupied by the parents. The second largest, also with a private bath, was assigned to ten-year-old Sally and her seven-year-old sister, Laura. Five-year-old Jimmy and three-year-old Bobby shared the third largest bedroom. The smallest became the private domain of thirteen-year-old David. The three boys shared the bathroom that opened out onto the hall.

Five years later the parents made the overnight trip to take David and his possessions off to college 400 miles away. They returned to discover Jimmy, now ten, had moved into the bedroom formerly occupied by David.

When David returned for a four-night visit over Thanksgiving, Jimmy agreed to return to his old place for those four days. David, however, was shocked to discover his remaining possessions piled in the closet and the walls covered with Jimmy's favorite posters and photographs.

"What have you done to my room?" stormed David, who had expected to find his old room exactly as he had left it three months earlier. "Who gave you the right to move all my stuff?"

"It's not your room," explained the unrepentant Jimmy. "It's now my place, and I've fixed it up the way I want it. Be sure you don't move any of my stuff while you're here!"

* * * * *

Three years later Sally left to attend the state university. Except for holiday visits, Laura now had her own room with her own private bath.

Two years later Laura was the valedictorian of her high

school graduating class of nearly 600 students. She also earned awards for outstanding performance in journalism, soccer, mathematics, and community service.

Several years earlier Laura had finalized her career plans. She wanted to be an engineer, like her father, but her plans were more extravagant. She was absolutely committed to going on to earn her doctorate in engineering.

The combination of her academic achievements plus her extracurricular activities, personality, and plans for graduate school made her an exceptionally attractive candidate. A few months before she graduated, she had been accepted by the three engineering schools at the top of her university shopping list. The top school on her list also offered a full-expense scholarship for two years with the possibility of extending it for her junior and senior years. That offer was matched by the other two schools.

Two days before the deadline for her response, an assistant dean, along with an admissions counselor, came to see Laura. The assistant dean came right to the point. "We want you to enroll in our school. You already have received our scholarship offer. We're here to sweeten the pot. A year ago the university decided to completely remodel an old dormitory that was constructed back in 1969. It is less than a half mile from our engineering school. The design for the remodeling consists largely of four-person suites, each with its own bathroom, but on each floor there also are two single rooms, each with its own private bath. One on each floor is reserved for the resident counselor. The other is available for student occupancy. We checked before we left this morning, and that other single room on the second floor is still available. The student housing department has agreed to hold it for us until tomorrow noon. It's yours if you want it. If you prefer, of course, you may choose one of those four-person suites. I should warn you, however, that those single rooms are the only ones that also have a reserved parking space to the rear of the building."

At this point Don Johnson began to explain why they had been looking favorably at the top school on Laura's list. Among other reasons, that was the engineering school from which he had graduated twenty-five years earlier.

Laura interrupted to declare, "Dad, I've made up my mind. This is the school I want to go to, and I'm looking forward to having my own private room."

Laura's grandfather had attended a one-room rural elementary school. While in the eighth grade, the grandfather's favorite uncle came by to see his school, meet the teacher, and offer the fourteen-year-old boy a ride to his parents' home a mile away. The boy proudly pointed out to his uncle his desk in the rear row. "This is my place," he declared. "I've been looking forward to this desk ever since I was in fifth grade. The back row is reserved for eighth graders, so two years ago I asked the teacher to reserve it for me when I became an eighth grader."

For the next fifteen minutes this youngster showed his uncle around what was now a nearly empty school building and finally took him for a walk around the playground. It became clear to the uncle that his nephew was completely at home in this environment.

A half century later a Florida professor wrote a book in which he explained how most adults need three places in their life. The first place is where they live. The second is where they work. The third is where they are identified by who they are as a person, not by their family ties or by their job.[14] For this eighth grader, that rural school was both his second and third place.

* * * * *

Over a period of two hours on a Monday morning, thirty-two adults arrive at a retreat center for a five-day workshop that will begin with the noon meal. As they register, a staff member explains, "One of us will take you to your room where you'll be sleeping this week. On the way we will show you the dining hall where we'll convene at a quarter to twelve."

* * * * *

The family of four gathers for the evening meal. The father sits in the same place he has occupied for years. The mother also sits in her place. The oldest child sits across the table from the younger sibling, an arrangement they have followed ever since the younger child graduated from the high chair.

When company is present, that seating arrangement is altered, but everyone feels a sense of relief after the company has departed and each member of the family can occupy his or her own place.

* * * * *

Twelve adults come together from all over the country for a one-day meeting scheduled for 9:00 A.M. to 4:00 P.M. The convenor knows all the other eleven. The covenor's colleagues know six of the eleven. The three oldest participants know one another as well as the covenor, but this is a first-time acquaintanceship with the remaining eight. The other seven know the convenor, but for four everyone else is a stranger.

A few minutes before nine, the three oldest members of the group go over and sit on one side of a long conference table. They assume the convenor will sit at one end. The three choose the side facing a long solid blank wall with a row of windows behind them. Across from them are seated two participants who are longtime friends, plus three other members of this ad hoc group. The convenor sits at one end. The colleague from headquarters sits at the other end.

One of the remaining two sits to the convenor's right, next to the three who picked their seats first. The twelfth participant arrives a few seconds later and takes the chair to the left of the convenor's colleague.

Ninety minutes later they take a fifteen-minute break and return promptly to the same chairs they had occupied earlier. Lunch is from 12:30 to 1:30. They return, and everyone goes immediately to what is now their familiar places. It is a pleasant and remarkably productive meeting, and everyone departs feeling this was a good investment of time, energy, and money. During the day no one either asked or offered to swap places at the table. In retrospect, by 9:30 it was clear that all twelve had staked out and filed their claims to their places. They all acted like normal grown-up human beings.

The Evolution of the American Public High School

* * * * *

A common experience for parents on a long trip is, after a rest stop, Johnny insists on sitting in the place in the back that had been occupied by Becky for the first few hours of the trip. "Johnny, you're a big kid. Quit acting like a child," admonishes a parent.

What Are the Alternatives?

One alternative is to ignore the importance of place in people's lives. A second is to pretend this is nonsense, or at least it does not apply to adolescents.

A third is to accept it as a fact, but given the space limitations of the large public school, make provisions for granting people the value and continuity of place only where this is really important. That short list might include an office for each administrator, a private room for the school nurse, one for the safety officer, one for the probation counselor, a teachers' lounge, possibly an office for each department chair, the locker room for athletes, a desk in a classroom for each teacher of an academic subject, a room for those working on the school newspaper, and a locker in a corridor for each student.

This would enable anyone interested in discovering the hierarchy of values that drive the decision-making processes in that school to do so by studying these responses to the natural human hunger for "my own place."

> **Anyone interested in discovering the hierarchy of values that drive the decision-making processes in [a] school [can] do so by studying [that school's] responses to the natural human hunger for "my own place."**

A fourth alternative is for every student to own a backpack and carry their place with them. This is what the United States

84

Army did in World War II when every enlisted person was issued a barracks bag.

A fifth alternative would be a public high school with an enrollment of 200 to 500 students meeting in a building designed to respond effectively to everyone's natural desire to have my own place.

A Step Up the Ladder

"You will always remember this night for the rest of your life," advised an uncle as he congratulated his nephew, who had graduated from high school on that early June evening in 1935. "You may never graduate again. This is a great accomplishment!" That eighteen-year-old young man had six uncles and two aunts on his father's side of the family tree and two uncles and five aunts on his mother's side. Like his father and mother, all of them were the American-born children of immigrant parents from central Europe. None of them had ever even attended high school. Eventually all but three of his cousins graduated from high school, but he was the first!

For this young man, high school was not a place to prepare for admission to college or to the state university. It was not a warehouse where he was stored until ready to go to work. He had been working an average of six hours a day on his father's dairy farm during the school year and twelve to fourteen hours daily during the summer. His preparation for life was largely accomplished on the farm.

For him, high school opened up whole new vistas for learning. He was challenged to become a lifelong learner by a dynamic principal, a science teacher, an athletic coach who rejected anything less than wholehearted effort, and two women on the faculty who believed their assignment was to make learning a pleasurable experience.

His uncle was correct. That was his last graduation. That eighteen-year-old boy became a full-time farmer. For him, high school was a ladder up into a world he had not known existed. He spent the next fifty-five years living in a world organized around that joy of learning. That also explains why he was a successful farmer! The basic generalization is the larger the size of the student body, the greater the degree of anonymity, the higher the level of institutional complexity, the more likely a large proportion of the students become increasingly bored with school and perceive it as resembling a warehouse. The smaller the size of the student body, the more unlikely it is for a teenager to spend four years there without at least one teacher taking a personal interest in that student and challenging him or her with the vision of what could be. The smaller the size of the school, the larger the proportion of students who perceive it to be a learning community and the smaller the proportion who perceive it to be a warehouse.

The ecological environment influences everyone's perceptions, attitudes, and behavior—and it is difficult to change that environment!

What Do You Believe?

At this point it is necessary to move the discussion to a more subjective topic. This observer is convinced that most policy-making decisions and much of human behavior are based on a perception of contemporary reality. What we believe affects what we do. This can be illustrated by three questions that are an essential part of the central thesis of this chapter and this book.

First, do you believe that most human beings find it to be relatively easy to engage in antisocial behavior that can escalate into violence?[15] On some occasions, this may be an act of revenge for an actual or fancied wrong. On other occasions, it may be a "follow the leader" sequence in which that antisocial behavior is modeled by one or more leaders and the followers find it easy to do what they would not do on their own initiative.

Examples include massacres during wartime, lynchings, road rage, gang rape, and a variety of mob actions.

On many occasions it is the senseless act of violence by an

individual who murders an innocent party while robbing a merchant or a retailer or in a drive-by shooting.

Far more frequently it is the use of "excessive force" in a basketball or football game or an intentional "beaning" in a baseball game or bullying younger or smaller students in the school years. The novel *The Lord of the Flies* suggests it is easy for children to engage in violent behavior.

Second, do you believe it is easier for an individual, or a group, to engage in extreme forms of antisocial behavior when confronted by someone whom it is easy to identify as "my enemy"? If you do not believe that, go read the accounts of the propaganda used to sway public opinion during wartime. Demonizing the enemy encourages violent behavior.

Third, do you believe it is easier for human beings to engage in extreme forms of antisocial behavior against people who are identified as "not one of us" or "not our kind of people"?

Examples to illustrate this point begin with the Holocaust and include slavery; "ethnic cleansing"; the rape and murder of prostitutes; World War II battles in the Pacific; lynchings; the seventeenth-, eighteenth-, and nineteenth- century attacks on Native Americans by persons with a Western European ancestry; and Kosovo, East Timor, and Grozny in 1999.

Those who put little credence in any of those statements will have little difficulty defending the environment created by the large public high school. Those who agree with those three belief statements will recognize the need to distinguish among the groups that populate the corridors, cafeterias, schoolyards, parking lots, and athletic fields of the large public high school.

Cliques, Teams, Groups, and Gangs

Here again we must begin with questions about contemporary reality.

Do you believe the most ancient and the most effective strategy for organizing a collection of individuals into a highly cohesive and unified group is to identify a common enemy and to organize those individuals against that common enemy?[16]

87

The Evolution of the American Public High School

Do you believe "winning" is an easier motivational tactic to use in reinforcing group identity and cohesiveness than is "doing good"? In other words, is it easier to organize a basketball team around the goal of defeating the opposing team than to recruit players for a game in which physical exercise is the primary purpose and no one will keep score?

Do you believe "birds of a feather tend to flock together" and that homogeneity is a more effective organizing principle than heterogeneity or diversity?

Do you believe that personal self-fulfillment can be an effective organizing principle to transform a collection of strangers into a closely knit and unified group, but that many participants may drop out before gaining a sense of belonging because this is a relatively slow process and requires highly competent leadership?

Most large public high schools allocate a substantial amount of money annually to subsidize the organization of students into closely knit groups. These efforts usually rely heavily on the first of the three organizing principles described here. They also include only a minority of the male students and an even smaller minority of female students. The names given to these organized groups include basketball teams, football teams, baseball teams, tennis teams, and soccer teams.

In most large public high schools far fewer resources are invested in the more difficult organizing principles required to help the majority of students "find a home" within a group where they can acquire the skills required to be an effective leader or experience the satisfaction derived from being a contributing member of a team or earn a higher level of self-confidence or gain an appreciation for the contributions of people who are "not like me."

One reason for that discrepancy, of course, is public support for a football team that wins the state championship in their division greatly exceeds the public support aroused when the high school newspaper is voted the best in the state.

What are the alternatives left for the students who either are not interested or not qualified to be on a varsity athletic team or serve as a cheerleader or work on the school newspaper or the yearbook or play in the band or sing in a vocal group or serve as an officer in the student government or participate in some other extracurricular activity?

One is to become a member of a clique or social network that has a relatively high degree of homogeneity among the participants.[17] A common unifying principle is, "Those are the kids who like to hang out together."

Cliques are created to fill a void in people's lives. If the ecological environment of the very large group does not provide adequate affirmation of an individual's worth, membership in a small group of five to fifteen people can fill that void. A high school's ecological environment can be designed to create a place for a large number of cohesive groups. Or it can be designed to create an informal need for a large number of exclusionary cliques. The larger the number of people in an institution, the more likely there will be a disproportionately large number of (a) exclusionary cliques and (b) alienated individuals identified as "loners." This is one reason why for over three thousand years the most effective military forces have been organized as a unified collection of cohesive small units usually composed of between five and seventeen persons.

The choice for the large public high school is to re-create itself as a collection of small, closely knit and cohesive groups or to exist with an unnecessarily high level of alienation within the student body. If the school is not organized to provide everyone with a range of attractive opportunities to gain a sense of belonging, the exclusionary cliques will fill that void.

If the teenagers perceive the school environment to be repressive, and if they feel alienated from the mainstream of the student body, it is relatively easy for them to organize a gang against a common enemy, which may be a rival gang or another ethnic group or a teacher or the school as an institution.

A third option is to go to class and try to survive without the fellowship and support of any kind of social network.

The Evolution of the American Public High School

What Is a Negative Ecological Environment?

The impact of the ecological environment on secondary education can be illustrated by a few examples.

1. The convicted felon is sentenced to a term of three years in prison. The type, name, and location of the prison is chosen, not by the convict who would prefer not to be in prison, but by distant authorities.

Every student in that private four-year liberal arts college has (a) chosen to enroll in college and (b) selected that particular school over other possibilities.

If a public high school is to fill the role as a college preparatory experience, should the students have a choice over (a) whether or not to enroll and (b) which high school among at least four or five possibilities will be their choice?

2. The physical design, operation, and schedule of a prison is to enhance safety, peace, security, predictability, and a good working environment for the paid staff. In some prisons, the authorities can predict weeks in advance, with a high degree of accuracy, which room a particular inmate will be occupying at a particular time of day.

That four-year private liberal arts college was designed to enhance a sense of community, to challenge students to discover and experience the joy of learning, to venture into the unknown, to fulfill their God-given potential, to improve their skills in meeting and making new friends, to gain new knowledge, and to become creative lifelong learners.

3. The higher the level of anonymity among the people in a particular setting, the more likely at least some of the participants will view others as strangers, rivals, aliens, intruders, "different from us," and perhaps even as enemies. The lower the level of anonymity, the more likely the participants will view others as acquaintances, colleagues, fellow pilgrims on a journey together, allies, and friends.

4. The pedagogical methodology and the content chosen by the teacher is to enhance the reputation of the school and staff. Therefore, a high priority is given to "teaching to the

90

(state-mandated) test," rather than to experience the joy of learning.

5. That priority to enhance the reputation of the school and the paid staff tolerates, and perhaps even encourages, cheating.

6. Rather than fulfillment and satisfaction from achieving excellence and a frequently expressed desire, "I wish we had more time to do this right," the ecological environment is dominated by such silent questions as, "How long before we can get out of here?" and "How many days until vacation?"

7. The top priority in determining the daily routine in a prison is the convenience and safety of the paid staff, not the preferences of the inmates.

The daily routine in an efficient and productive factory is influenced by cost-benefits ratios, maximizing the use of expensive machinery, and meeting production deadlines. An 11:00 P.M. to 7:00 A.M. work shift may not match the biological clock of the employees on that shift, but it is essential to making a profit.

The efficient operation of a profitable warehouse includes an efficient floor plan, a high degree of predictability in schedules, a completely passive role for what is stored there, and a safe and secure physical environment for the employees.

At least a few institutions of higher education give students substantial control over their daily class schedules and even their mealtimes.

Which would be the appropriate model for a high school that identifies itself as a college preparatory school?

8. A growing number of employers place a high value on employee participation in decision making, on rewarding workers for suggestions on how to improve the system, and on employees working as teams.

Should the public high school prepare students for employment in that environment? Or should students be prepared to work in an environment in which most policies are made by distant authorities, tradition drives the decision-making processes, and the system rewards individual performance?

9. A reasonable estimate is that out of every 100 ninth graders who will enroll in a public high school in the fall of

2001, approximately 85 will receive a diploma forty-five months later. Out of those 85, approximately 50 will enroll in an institution of higher education. Out of those 50, a generous estimate is that 25 will be fully prepared to do college-level work successfully without any remedial courses or special tutoring. The other 50 either will drop out before graduation or not go on to college.

A required ninth-grade class in English composition is designed for 25 students. The same teacher offers five sections of that required English composition class every day. Is it reasonable to expect that the one lesson plan the teacher will prepare for the day will be appropriate for (a) all five classes, (b) those ninth graders who four years later will be enrolling in college, (c) those who will drop out before graduation, and (d) those who will graduate and go directly into the labor force?

10. That huge billboard out in front of the school, designed to be read by a passing motorist, exalts the championships won by the school's athletic teams. It conveys the impression that this is a huge factory that exists to produce winning sports teams.

It does not celebrate the graduation rate for the entering ninth-grade class of four years earlier. It does not lift up the names of the teenagers who are straight-A students. It does not report the proportion of graduating seniors who have earned scholarships to prestigious colleges and universities. It does not report the success of dropouts who have become successful members of the local labor force. It does not celebrate the achievements of the graduates of two or three years earlier.

That billboard appears to be designed to provide a daily reminder to every student that this institution is organized around success on the athletic field, not around academic achievement in the classroom. That could be justified if 80 or 90 percent of the students were members of these winning sports teams.

What Is the Issue?

The basic generalization is: the larger the number of people in a social setting, the easier it is to feel like an outsider. When two people lunch together, each is engaged in the conversation. When three people serve on a special task force created to recommend a solution to a problem, all three usually will work together to come up with a recommendation all three can support. When twelve people eat together, the Bible suggests that sooner or later one will betray the leader and one will deny ever having known that leader. When twenty people serve on a special task force, it is easy for three or four to disclaim any ownership of what was presented as a unanimous recommendation. When that two-hour seminar includes seven people, it is easy for at least five or six to be active participants. When that history class includes thirty-five students, it is easy for three or four to dominate the discussion and for fifteen to be completely silent for the entire period.

The larger the number of people in a social setting, the easier it is to feel like an outsider.

This leads to two questions.

First, is it the responsibility of the policy makers in the large public high school to design a learning environment that encourages or discourages active participation by the students? Or is that the responsibility of the teachers? Or of the students? Or is the dissemination of information a far higher priority? Can teaching occur without learning?

Second, should the large public high school be expected to design a collection of extracurricular activities that will include every student in at least one carefully organized group or team or board that is designed to achieve at least ten of these sixteen goals: (1) experience the satisfactions of helping others with no direct benefit to oneself; (2) help teenagers enhance their skills in meeting and making new friends; (3) challenge all participants to do what they know they cannot do; (4) experience the positive contributions from people "who are not like me"; (5) learn how to function as a contributing member of a team (a drama group, a rowing crew, a soccer team, and a three-student team in a physics class are excellent examples); (6) improve at least one skill area of every participant; (7) model high standards of ethical behavior; (8) transmit to adolescents traditional "American" moral values; (9) discover the satisfactions that are the reward for excellence; (10) experience the positive dimensions of "winning"; (11) fulfill, with the appropriate advance training, the role of "leader" or "president" or "chairperson" or "coach" (the Mormons excel at this); (12) experience failure and discover how to recover from it (the 1995 film *Mr. Holland's Opus* is a superb example of this); (13) discover and enjoy the freedom that is the reward for placing deferred gratification ahead of immediate satisfaction in a personal value system (complete the homework before going to the party); (14) experience the feeling "I know I belong because I know I am needed"; (15) enjoy the support of caring friends; and, most important of all, (16) develop a friendship with an adult who merits the respect and admiration of adolescents?

Is this a fair expectation to place on every high school? Or should that be the responsibility of other voluntary associations, such as summer baseball teams, churches, summer soccer league, Scouting, 4-H Clubs, service clubs and lodges, or the local park district?

Or should those goals be realized in the off-campus work experience of teenagers?

Or should the primary responsibility be placed on parents?

The answers to these three questions will suggest whether the appropriate model for a high school in the twenty-first century is a warehouse or a factory or a prison or a learning community.

Three Choices

How can the hostility and alienation that lead to violence be defused? In a remarkably thoughtful and constructive essay, a former high school principal has suggested making the culture of the school community friendlier, less threatening, and more rewarding. He has described several constructive steps to achieving that goal.[18]

From a larger perspective, this raises a fundamental question: What is possible?

Experience suggests it is extremely difficult to change the culture of a large institution without first changing the ecological environment. That includes rewriting the rule book as well as transforming the physical environment and the social settings. The transformation of the contemporary large public high school also will require clarifying the expectations projected for each school, designing pedagogical methodologies that are consistent with those expectations, and broad-based agreement on the criteria for evaluation.

Automobile manufacturers have abandoned older assembly plants and constructed new ones as part of a large goal of transforming the culture and improving productivity. Hospitals have razed a relatively new wing in order to house a new system of patient care. States have replaced older prisons that were designed as places of incarceration with new structures designed to reduce antisocial behavior and promote rehabilitation. Colleges and universities have remodeled or replaced the old-style dormitories with new ones designed to enhance the residents' skills in interpersonal relationships. Success often requires a new physical environment, the creation of a new institutional culture, a completely new rule book, and frequently replacing some of the players who are unable or unwilling to abandon the old traditions, precedents, culture, and rule book.

Changing the culture of the large public high school without changing the ecological environment is more than a huge challenge. It is an impossible dream.

An easier course of action is to change the ecological environment in order to create a new school community culture. One current example is to house five or six different high schools in a building constructed in the early 1990s to house one high school with 2,500 students.

The easiest road to offering the students a friendlier, more supportive, less threatening, and more challenging school community is to make a fresh start. That is one of the driving forces behind the current charter school movement.[19] This movement usually calls for a new game with a new rule book, new players, and a new culture of learning.

Chapter Five

WHERE DO YOU FIND QUALITY?

W here do you see an emphasis on quality in your high school?" This is one of several questions I have directed to high school students during the past three decades.

Before looking at the responses to that question, it should be pointed out that the teenagers I interview do not constitute a representative cross-section of American youth. My sample includes, in disproportionately large numbers, adolescents who (1) are descendants of Western European ancestors, (2) come from families that rank in the top 75 percent of the American population in socioeconomic terms, (3) are being reared by Protestant churchgoing parents, (4) expect to graduate from high school, with the vast majority planning to go on to college or to a university, (5) rank in the upper half of their class academically, (6) participate in extracurricular activities in school, and (7) are members of the high school youth group in their church. In other words, these are the adolescents most public high schools originally were designed to serve.

Where do these teenagers perceive a high emphasis on quality in their high school?

The most frequent response is competitive interscholastic athletic teams, such as football and basketball. In one group of eighteen students representing three different high schools, every hand went up when I asked, "Is that number one in your school?" At that point, one somnolent senior interrupted to explain to this naive old gentleman, "Even the dummies know the answer to that question."

97

A distant second in frequency of responses is, "Band." A close third is that teacher, usually a male, who is perceived by the students to be an independent, maverick-type personality, who demands the very best from the most promising students, but also projects relatively high expectations of the rest of the class. "If he believes you have talent, he demands quality from you!"

Fourth in frequency are extracurricular activities, such as working on the school newspaper or the yearbook or serving as a cheerleader or as a member of a vocal music group.

A close fifth is the advanced-placement class. When these are mentioned, frequently one or more of the teenagers dissent. "If you do your homework, pay attention, and don't let yourself get behind in the assignments, the advanced-placement classes in my school are a fairly easy A, and at worse a guaranteed B."

Finally, a small number of juniors or seniors will make sure that I understand there is at least one academic course in their school that does emphasize quality. This is usually chemistry, physics, biology, or a math class, but after a couple of minutes others will explain that is because that particular teacher projects very high expectations.

A Larger Worldview

When I next broaden the question to include their life outside high school, four responses dominate the subsequent discussions. For those for whom this is appropriate, the emphatic number-one response is, "The fast food restaurant where I work." For many of the boys, the number-one place to look for quality is in motor vehicles and especially in the television ads for cars. A substantial proportion of the girls and a few of the boys insist "clothes" should be at or near the top of that list. Once or twice a year someone will add, "My mom" or "My dad" to the list. When that happens, it is not uncommon for that nomination to be affirmed, "Yep! Your dad should be at the top of your list." Once in a while a teenager will mention a popular contemporary music group, but only rarely does that nomination elicit broad support. One fifteen-year-old explained, "My dad's a tool-and-die maker. He says if you want to see an emphasis on high quality, come to the shop where he works."

After interviews with over two thousand students, it is worth noting that in response to this follow-up question, I have never heard "television," and I have heard "my church" only twice.

One of the values of these group conversations and of one-to-one interviews is to distinguish what one cohort says from what is stated by another cohort. For example, I have heard many high school administrators and school board members brag about the "quality of our faculty." I have listened to an even larger number of parents boast of the exceptionally high quality and the many features of that new $20 to $50 million building that was just completed to house their local public high school. Many even refer to it as "our high school."

By contrast, the students appear to respond from a conceptual framework in which the definition of the term "high school" includes the student body, the culture of that institution, the many adults who are paid to work there, and extracurricular activities. Therefore, it is not surprising that, when I ask where they see an emphasis on quality, about the only comment related to the real estate that I ever hear concerns the absence of adequate parking space for student-owned motor vehicles or that the lockers are too small or are crowded together so it is difficult to gain access to one's own storage space. The common answer to the locker problem is a bigger backpack. The answer to the parking problem is the $50 monthly fee to park in the driveway of a nearby residence.

The students' perception of contemporary reality when the subject under discussion is the large public high school has only a modest degree of overlap with the perception that drives the decision-making processes of administrators, school board members, and parents. (The omission of teachers from that paragraph is intentional!)

These group conversations with high school students usually involve somewhere between ten and two dozen teenagers and usually run for thirty to seventy-five minutes.

The Evolution of the American Public High School

A Parent's Perspective

Occasionally I meet someone on the following day who, as part of the introductions, says, "Last night you met my son (or daughter)." That motivates me to inquire, "Well, what did your youngster tell you about our time together?" I am deeply interested in the worldview of today's teenagers, so I eagerly pursue every opportunity to learn. A typical conversation goes something like this:

Schaller: Yes, I remember Terry. You should be proud of such an articulate and reflective youngster. What was Terry's version of what happened last evening?

Parent: First of all, I had to exert an above-average amount of parental pressure to persuade Terry to skip television to come to your meeting, but I had some peer allies, so that helped.

Schaller: After Terry came home, what did you hear?

Parent: I began by asking how it went. I expected to hear, "Another boring meeting." Instead I was told it was a "great" meeting. So I asked, "If it was so great, what happened?" Terry explained, "All we did was this guy asked questions, listened, asked more questions, and listened. He never told us what to do, nor did he ever tell us whether we gave the right or wrong answers to his questions. I learned a lot as I listened to what the other kids said."

Schaller: That's a fair description of our hour together. My only regret is we ran out of time before we had a chance to deal with some follow-up questions.

Parent: That's what Terry told us, that the time went by real fast. When I asked what made it such a great meeting if all you did was interrogate the kids, Terry explained. "For most of us it was the first time an adult ever asked us for our opinion, listened, took seriously what we said, and never made any judgmental comments about our answer." I'm glad you thought it was important for you to meet with those kids.

100

It is important to measure, or to hear firsthand, what teenagers perceive about the world they inhabit. By doing that, what teenagers say becomes important.

Chapter 6 points out that we measure what we believe is important. Subsequently, what we measure becomes important. I believe it is important to measure, or to hear firsthand, what teenagers perceive about the world they inhabit. By doing that, what teenagers say becomes important.

Chapter Six

IS IT A DYSFUNCTIONAL SYSTEM?

What is the best way to create a dysfunctional organization? One effective strategy is to load a variety of incompatible goals, tasks, expectations, and responsibilities onto a healthy institution. Another is to create a new organization with mutually incompatible goals. A third is to create a subversive internal reward system that undermines the original purpose of that institution.

The large American public high school is a victim of all three strategies. In the closing years of the nineteenth century, an influential, well organized, and articulate group of progressive educators argued that the public high school should prepare students for admission to college. A larger, but less influential, group contended that the primary purpose should be to prepare students for life. An overlapping group emerged to declare that the real need was to prepare students for entrance into the paid labor force. A good apprentice would benefit from at least two years of high school training.

While rarely stated this bluntly, as suggested in chapter 2, that explosive growth in enrollment during the first several decades of the twentieth century also could be attributed, at least in part, to the disappearance of jobs for youngsters in their mid-teens. The public high school became a place to store restless adolescents until they could enter the labor force.

Six other characteristics of the dysfunctional organization merit a word here. The first is denial. Typically the leaders in the dysfunctional organization deny that "we have a problem."

Is It a Dysfunctional System?

Second, the temptation is to personify and identify the person(s) who created the problem.

Overlapping that is the reluctance or inability to look at flaws in the system. The statement that systems produce what they are designed to produce arouses negative responses. If most high school students are bored, it clearly is their fault. "Our system is not designed to produce boredom!" "Our system is not designed to place jocks at the top of the student deference pyramid."

During the summer of 1999 several high school principals and boards of education declared, "Our top priority is safety. We will do whatever is necessary to provide a safe environment for our students and teachers." A fourth characteristic of the dysfunctional organization is when a means-to-an-end moves ahead of purpose in the ordering or priorities. Public schools should be organized around learning, not safety!

"That's the way we've always done it here" frequently is a fifth sign of the dysfunctional organization. Local tradition moves ahead of purpose, goals, and creativity in decision making. The leaders keep doing the same things year after year, but they expect different results.

A sixth common characteristic of the dysfunctional organization was described earlier in chapter 4. That is a disregard for the importance of place in peoples' lives.

An Adult Employment Center

As the years rolled by, public high schools gradually evolved into attractive employment centers. One reason, of course, was the Great Depression of the 1930s, which created a scarcity of decent indoor jobs that did not require heavy lifting, paid a reasonable salary, and were open to women.

One of the notable changes in the tax-supported common schools of the nineteenth century was the gradual increase in the number of women employed as teachers. One part of the explanation was the migration of young adult males who followed the frontier to the west. This created a surplus of young unmarried women back east. One solution to that problem was to allow women to teach in the elementary schools. Perhaps more important were the efforts of Catherine Beecher, Horace Mann, and others who contended that women would naturally be more effective teachers than men.

One argument was that school should be seen as an extension of the home and, therefore, teaching was naturally a maternal function. A second argument was that a school should transmit qualities such as affection, refinement, manners, moralism, and culture, and women could do that more effectively than men. A third argument was that women would teach for a lower salary than demanded by men.[1] Thus the comparatively low salaries for teachers, the relatively low status of teachers in the culture, and the tendency of men to use teaching as an entry point into the labor force also were factors opening the door for women to teach in both elementary and secondary schools.

Up through the 1930s teaching, along with work as a telephone operator, clerk typist, receptionist, secretary, nurse, sales clerk, seamstress, or domestic servant were among the few paid vocations open to women.

One result of opening the doors to women to teach in the public schools was a greatly expanded potential labor force. Thus after World War II, when the demand began to rise for specialists on the payroll of the public high schools, women were there to help meet that demand.

A concurrent change was the sharp increase in the number of jobs as the public high schools increased in size.

In 1960, for example, the public secondary schools reported an enrollment of 13 million students and employed 550,000 teachers for an average of one teacher per 24 students. Thirty years later the public secondary school enrollment had increased by 18 percent to 15,412,000, and the number of teachers had increased by 84 percent to 1,012,000. The new ratio was one teacher to 15 students.

The number of administrators and support staff nearly tripled between 1960 and 2000.

Is It a Dysfunctional System?

More important, however, was a more subtle change as public school teaching evolved from a calling or vocation in the 1930s into a job by the end of the twentieth century. (See chapter 12 for an elaboration of this point.)

This combination of the increase in the number of people on the payroll of the large public high schools plus the evolution from vocation to job plus the natural tendency to drift into a bureaucratic mode produced several predictable consequences.

One of these is that the large public high school now serves as an adult employment center.[2] In many districts a huge amount of time and money must be invested in an effort to dismiss an incompetent teacher. It often is cheaper to assign the incompetent teacher to a made-up job and hire a replacement than to dismiss that teacher.

In recent years several state legislatures have adopted legislation that makes it financially attractive for public school teachers to retire at age fifty-five. The old role as an adult employment center has been expanded to an adult employment and early retirement center. One characteristic of the dysfunctional organization is when it encourages its very best employees to retire early.

A third consequence is that the salary schedule for faculty and administrators has become one of the basic indicators for the evaluation of a public school system and for choosing between a separate high school district versus a unified K-12 system. It also is worth noting that in several states fewer than one-half of all dollars spent on public education for grades K-12 is allocated to classroom staff.

A fourth is that the schedule may be designed for the convenience of the employees, rather than to create a positive learning environment. In one large unified K-12 public school district, the schedule for the high school students is determined by the schedules of the part-time bus drivers. One fleet of school buses is used to transport elementary, middle, and high school students to their respective schools. That means high school classes must begin early so those drivers and buses will be available to transport younger students later in the morning.

That schedule is contrary to mounting evidence that the internal biological clocks of adolescents call for a later morning time for beginning the day's activities.[3]

It is not uncommon in the dysfunctional organization for the convenience of the employees to drive the schedule.

A few years ago one northern state experienced a record number of blizzards. One result was that most schools were closed on many winter days and could not meet the minimum number of days required to be eligible for state aid. The state legislature passed a bill that declared a school district could make up that deficit of days by being open for additional days at the end of the normal school year. The teachers would be required to be present on all of those make-up days, but the students would not be expected to attend.

Back in the 1930s the salary of the public high school principal was approximately 160 to 200 percent of the salary for the beginning high school teacher. Today it is more likely to be triple or quadruple. That opens the door to another facet of the dysfunctional institution.

What Is the Reward System?

A public investigation of a scandal in the athletic department of the University of Minnesota in 1999 revealed that the president of that great university was being paid $250,000 a year. The total compensation package for the head coach of the basketball team was $700,000 annually.

The American labor market offers a beginning annual salary of $16,000 to $70,000 for most college and university graduates. One exception is the basketball or football or baseball star who may receive a multimillion dollar bonus simply for signing a professional sports contract, which also pays a very high annual salary.

If the central purpose of the public high school is to (a) prepare those who plan to go on to school for college or university and/or to (b) prepare students for life and/or to (c) prepare students to enter the paid labor force and/or to (d) help parents socialize adolescents into the American culture, then a reasonable expectation would be that the compensation of the adults would be related to how effectively they helped to fulfill that central purpose.

The most remarkable, and until recently unchallenged, expression of dysfunctionalism is in the reward system for academic achievement. The typical public school salary schedule rewards teachers—and sometimes even administrators—for academic achievement. Earning a master's degree or a doctorate is rewarded with an increase in compensation. The typical public high school salary schedule, however, does not reward teachers for the academic achievement of students or for enabling them to learn to excel.[4]

In a few schools, athletic coaches are rewarded for the success of their varsity teams. That, however, stands out as one of the few examples that call for adults to be rewarded for student performance.

That reward system was challenged in the fall of 1999 when the Denver public school system created a small-scale, two-year pilot project to test the possibility of rewarding teachers for the academic achievements of their students.

If the central purpose is to provide tenured employment for adults, it is reasonable to expect that title, tenure, and academic credentials will be more influential than talent or student performance in determining compensation.

How Do You Evaluate?

Professionals with expertise in the evaluation of large organizations delivering person-centered services declare, sometimes with an excessive degree of self-confidence: If you can agree on the answer to these three questions, we can provide the criteria that will enable you to measure your performance:

Can you agree on the identity of your number-one or primary constituency?
Can you agree on what you are attempting to do with or for that primary constituency?

Can you agree on the basic assumptions guiding your decision-making constituency and in designing the services you provide to that constituency?

Adequate responses are relatively easy to secure to these three questions when the focus is on medical research. Thus far it has been impossible to secure useful responses when the focus is on educational research.

One characteristic of the dysfunctional organization is the absence of widely agreed upon and clearly defined criteria for self-evaluation.

Who Are the Victims?

"You're asking me if I approve of boys wearing baseball caps in my classroom?" challenged a ninth-grade teacher. "The answer is absolutely not!"

"Well, I see boys wearing baseball caps in your classroom," I pointed out. "If you do not approve, how come they're wearing them?"

"There is a limit on what I can do unilaterally," replied the teacher. "The only way we teachers could enforce such a rule would be if we all agreed to it and if the principal backed us or if the board of education adopted a dress code—and that probably would lead to a lawsuit. I did persuade all the other teachers to agree on a common standard on shoes. We adopted the slogan, 'No shoes, no seat,' so if a student comes to class barefoot, we have to admit them, but we can make them stand in the back of the room for the whole period."

* * * * *

Most public school teachers are required to have completed four or more years of college or university training. There they are exposed to a pedagogical model that emphasizes (a) individualism, (b) academic content, and (c) the transmission of knowledge from the learned to the unlearned. Typically one professor teaches two or three or four courses in his or her academic specialty. Graduate

108

assistants may lead discussion sections and grade papers, but, as in golf, the individual is the star. The caddies, or graduate assistants, are not perceived as valuable members of the team. The higher that school is on the prestige ladder of institutions of higher education, the more likely the model rewards individual research, administration, and lighter teaching workloads. The award-winning books by scholars usually have the name of an individual author on the cover, not the names of a team of five to seven people. Academic promotions reward the individual achievement of the teacher, not the academic achievements of the students.

After four or five years in that scholarly environment, the graduate leaves to go and teach in a large public high school. That probably also is organized by academic departments and is a lower-level model of the undergraduate school in the university. The candidates for teaching jobs are evaluated, at least in part, by their academic credentials. Many eventually have their own classroom with a passing parade of students coming into and leaving that classroom every period. The teacher is the emperor of that small domain. "What the other teachers do in their classroom is their business, not mine." A few of the teachers may earn a doctorate in their academic specialty and leave to teach in a college. Many, many more will use that teaching position as an entry into the labor force and go into some other vocation. Others will marry out of teaching or go into full-time educational administration. The reward system makes it clear that administration is valued more highly than performance in the classroom. That whole picture is consistent with the purpose of the public high school to provide attractive employment opportunities for university-educated adults. The reward system also makes it clear that individual performance is valued more highly than the performance of a teaching team.

How Long Is the List?

Let us pretend for a few minutes that among the top reasons for spending more than $100 billion annually on public high schools are these seventeen goals:

The Evolution of the American Public High School

1. To prepare a majority of the students for admission into the college or university of their choice.
2. To challenge teenagers to discover and repeatedly experience the joy of learning.
3. To socialize adolescents into a culture largely owned and operated by adults.
4. To provide attractive adult role models of loyal, well-informed, and socially valuable citizens who believe in the values of a democratic society.
5. To equip every student with minimal levels of competence in language and numerical skills and in the capability to comprehend simple abstract concepts.
6. To provide surrogate-parent figures for youth who have been reared in a dysfunctional home environment.
7. To channel into socially acceptable expressions the natural instincts of many adolescent males to express their feelings through violence, to seek power, to strive for power over others, to be recognized as a leader, to compete against their peers, to engage in high-risk behavior, and to win the affirmation of both peers and adults.
8. To provide positive and challenging alternative paths to learning for teenagers in rebellion against their parents' culture.
9. To offer socially and legally acceptable responses to the "raging hormone" problem.
10. For those who have not acquired this skill earlier, to learn how to meet and make new friends.
11. To provide a variety of attractive and socially acceptable avenues for an adolescent to experience meaningful relationships with peers through continuing membership in a group.
12. To discover and appreciate that the differences among people can be an asset rather than a liability.
13. To prepare adolescents to become contributing members of the American labor force.
14. To expose teenagers to the fact that marriage can be a healthy, happy, and enduring experience for most adults.[5]
15. To provide every student with the opportunity, the resources, and the support system required to experience suc-

cess in one facet of life; to be able to declare, "In that area of life I excel over 90 percent of my peers."

16. To experience the joy of being a contributing member of a team for which the focus is not on athletic performance, but on group learning and/or on helping others and/or accomplishing a meaningful task. Band, a vocal music group, membership on the editorial board of the school annual, the production of a television program, community service, and planning a three-day class trip are examples. Can classroom learning also be a team experience?

17. To create an ecological environment staffed with adults who are deeply committed to and enthusiastic about their vocation. The combination of that ecological environment and those adult role models will inspire 5 percent of the best students in each class to dream, "I would love to spend most of my adult life teaching in a high school like this one."

Four quick observations must be made about this list. First, it is far from complete. The reader is invited to expand it. Second, the rank order in importance will vary tremendously from one student to another. Third, the acceptable language for stating each of these purposes will vary from individual to individual. Fourth, that is a long list! Does that represent an excessively heavy burden to place on one institution? Which is the number one priority?

Why should we build such a list?

The most obvious explanation is that it helps to understand why teachers should be included on the list of victims of the current high school culture. One way for any system to produce a high level of frustration is to place an excessively long list of expectations on the participants.[6] A second is to design in it an absence of clarity on the rank order of importance of those many expectations. "The priorities vary with the situation, the time of day, the client, and what happened yesterday. You figure it out."

A third way to design a system to produce a high level of frustration is to identify several different clients, each of whom is the number-one client and each of whom brings a different set of expectations to the discussion on purpose.[7]

In many large public high schools the system is designed to produce a high level of frustration among the teachers. Systems produce what they are designed to produce. Dysfunctional systems tend to produce frustration, alienation, dropouts, hostility, adversarial relationships, and violence.

> **In many large public high schools the system is designed to produce a high level of frustration among the teachers.**

Another reason to look at that list is that with the possible exception of items 1, 2, 10, 11, and 12, most colleges and universities do little to prepare prospective teachers for that list of challenges.

Is That List Incomplete?

At this point a few readers may interrupt to point out that the list of seventeen expectations is far from complete. What widely shared expectations were overlooked? Should that list be expanded to include an additional dozen?

18. To serve as a therapy center for emotionally troubled teenagers?

19. To serve as a farm club for college and university football, basketball, and baseball teams?

20. To help adolescents avoid becoming addicted to hard drugs, alcohol, and tobacco?

21. To warehouse teenagers who do not want to be in school or in the labor force?

22. To serve as a recruitment center for the four branches of the military services?

23. To be a major player in the effort to eliminate white racism?

24. To help assimilate teenage immigrants into American society? (In the nineteenth century the labor force was the primary channel for accomplishing that goal.)

25. To prevent teenage girls from becoming pregnant?

26. To try and punish teenagers who engage in severely anti-social behavior? (Between 1985 and 1999 the number of juveniles arrested increased by 50 percent. The United States Department of Justice now offers grants to help finance the operation of teen courts. Most of these are housed in public high schools. Should the public high school serve as an extension of the criminal justice system?)

27. To provide an after-school custodial service for teenagers who cannot return home until late afternoon?

28. To operate a cafeteria that provides attractive, nutritious meals for teenagers once or twice a day? Or to encourage obesity?

29. To prevent anyone, except for safety officers, from bringing weapons into the school building?

Is it realistic to expect that all of those expectations can be fulfilled day after day by one institution under one roof?

Most highly trained professionals have earned, or at least claimed, the right to say, "I don't do that." The accountant does not design bridges. The cardiologist does not treat asthma. The computer programmer does not do brain surgery. The civil engineer does not do estate planning. The airline pilot does not serve drinks.

The high school teacher often is expected to do everything on those two lists plus other duties, such as being adviser to the school newspaper or taking tickets at the basketball games.

Are Summer Vacations Necessary?

A common suggestion today for improving the quality of public education is to increase the length of the school year from 180 to 220 days. Among the arguments for a nine-month school year are that (a) the youth are needed during the summer to help on the farm, (b) the teachers need the time to go to summer school to acquire more academic credentials, (c) the high summer temperatures are not conducive to effective classroom learning experiences, and (d) the administration needs two or three months to clean, repair, and renovate the buildings and prepare them for intensive use during the school year.

The Evolution of the American Public High School

Today migrants do much of the agricultural summer work formerly done by teenagers, and air conditioning is available to counter the summer heat.

A growing number of state legislatures have approved proposals that make it financially attractive for veteran teachers to retire at age fifty-five. Why would a school district want to replace its most experienced teachers with inexperienced candidates fresh out of school?

A useful conceptual framework for discussing the length of the school year and related issues came out of World War II. World War I had taught that "in peacetime abnormal men break down from normal stress, in wartime normal men break down from abnormal stress."[8] Twenty-five years later the British reported that their riflemen in North Africa experienced an average effective span of 400 combat days, twice the average for the Americans. After a total of 214 or fewer days in combat, *all* American infantrymen in the Mediterranean theater fell into one of five categories: (a) killed, (b) wounded, (c) lost due to physical sickness, (d) captured by the enemy, or (e) psychologically unfit for combat duty.

The conclusion was that the difference between the British experience and the American record was that the British pulled their men out of combat for a four-day rest after twelve days of continuous combat duty. The Americans, by contrast, usually were kept on continuous combat duty for twenty to eighty days before receiving a brief leave. The eventual compromise called for a maximum cumulative total of 180 days of combat to be served by any rifleman.[9]

Conversations with both teachers and students strongly suggest that for many of them, their daily life in the large public high school is a stress-producing experience. That is a normal, natural, and predictable product of a dysfunctional environment.

If the metaphor for the contemporary large public high school is combat rather than a warehouse or a prison, then the 180-day school year is consistent with precedents. If the high school students are discharged after four or five years of duty, it is reasonable to argue that the teachers should be pensioned off with an honorable discharge after thirty years of service.

An alternative possibility would be to shift from the metaphor of armed combat to that of the learning community in designing the social, physical, pedagogical, cultural, and ecological environment of the public high school.

So who are the primary victims in those public high schools that have evolved into dysfunctional systems? From this observer's perspective, the rank order is students, teachers, parents, future employers, principals, taxpayers, and college and university faculty who concentrate on teaching first- and second-year students. Many of the people in these seven categories claim that they should rank number one or two on this list of victims.

Chapter Seven

WHAT DAY IS IT?

Before looking at alternative courses of action for those who are dissatisfied with the public schools in general and the large public high schools in particular, it may be useful to take a brief detour and look at three facets of the context for reform. The political, social, economic, and cultural contexts have been transformed. Several changes constitute one facet of the context for reform and merit discussion here.

From Producer to Consumer

The first has been a change in the definition of the number-one client for tax-supported services. The combination of the Great Depression and the New Deal launched the beginning of a new era. The old tradition called for subsidizing the producer of services. The county home or "poor house" or veterans' home was replaced by direct financial aid to widows and to families with dependent children and, most expensive of all, by Social Security. The old synonym for "poor" was "poor widow." The new synonym is "young child."

Subsequently, the G.I. Bill of Rights was adopted by Congress in 1944, over the objections of the presidents of several elite universities. The veteran received a tax-subsidized voucher that could be used at the student's choice of school, public or private, secular or religious.

A persuasive argument can be made that two of the most successful public-policy decisions made by the United States

What Day Is It?

Congress in the twentieth century were the Social Security program to reduce poverty among the elderly and the G.I. Bill of Rights to greatly expand the number of well-educated members of the American labor force and to increase the number of families owning their own home.

Both programs were created to use tax funds to subsidize the consumer rather than the producer of services.

The Medicare legislation adopted in 1965 was a more recent move in the direction of subsidizing the consumer rather than the producer of tax-supported services.

One important exception was the public housing legislation of 1949 and later years, which directed the subsidies to the producers of the services—a policy that led to many disasters. Subsequently Section 8 vouchers represented the policy of subsidizing the consumer.

The Pell grants to college and university students also followed the public policy of subsdizing the consumer rather than the producer of tax-supported services.

Another exception has been the federal policy on subsidies that go to the producers of food and fiber (not services) and that, like public housing, produced less than ideal results. In recent years an amount equal to nearly one-half of all net farm income has come from the federal treasury, with many of the benefits accuring to the processors, rather than to either the producers or the consumers of food.

At this point a crucial distinction between vouchers and charter schools must be emphasized. Both expand the range of educational choices available to parents and children. Charter schools, like the public schools, are designed to provide a tax-funded financial subsidy to the producer of educational services. Vouchers provide a tax-funded subsidy to the consumer. Which principle do you believe will have the greatest political support from parents in 2005?

The consumers of tax-supported public services are becoming increasingly demanding, articulate, and politically influential.

117

What Do Employers Expect?

A second trend is the rising expectations employers project of new employees. A strong back and a powerful work ethic no longer are sufficient for securing a good job. Employers now want people who can read, comprehend, adapt, and write, who are comfortable with numbers, who bring a strong work ethic, and, most important of all, who are eager to learn.

Millions of immigrants with a limited level of formal education have come to the United States and have become productive and valued members of the labor force. They brought with them a strong work ethic, a passion to learn, a value system that placed deferred gratification above immediate satisfactions, and a skill (carpenter, seamstress, mechanic, gardener, keyboarder, welder, housekeeper, jeweler, tailor, janitor, painter, roofer, etc.).

Do today's employers have a right to expect that the candidate for a job who left high school with a low level of competence in reading, writing, arithmetic, and the ability to comprehend abstract concepts will offset that by bringing a strong work ethic, a desire to learn, and a marketable skill?

Employers have become some of the most influential of all of the constituencies served by the large public high schools.

New Generations

A third trend is that the students who graduated from the public high school in the era before 1950 and their parents are moving to retirement centers, nursing homes, and cemeteries. They represent the last generations who were satisfied with the public school system that served them. Successive generations are more discontented with the old ways of doing things, and many are open to radical changes in the institutions of our society. This can be seen in our political systems, in the role of labor unions, in telephone service, in entertainment, in transportation, in the churches, in housing, in dress codes, and in the increase in the number of people who work out of their homes, to name a few. These new generations also are more likely to be discontented with traditional educational systems for four-year-olds, for fourteen-year-olds, and for twenty-year-olds.

Americans born in the first third of the twentieth century were reared in the most patriotic era in this nation's history. They were taught that they had a moral obligation to serve and to be grateful and loyal to such institutions as the armed forces, service clubs, lodges, churches, denominations, veterans' organizations, political parties, colleges and universities, labor unions, employers, and the public schools. They applauded the challenge of President John F. Kennedy, "Ask not what your country can do for you, ask what you can do for your country."

Their children and grandchildren have been reared in a culture that has taught them that institutions exist, not to be served by volunteers, but to be sensitive and responsive to the needs of their constituents. "Customer service" is the new criterion for evaluating an institution, including the public school system.

Death is the number-one enemy of the status quo.

Overlapping that is a change in family constellations as families become smaller. As recently as the early 1970s the typical high school student body included a large proportion of middle-born children. As a group, middle-born children tend to have accumulated many years of experience getting along with people who are different from themselves. They tend to be extroverted and person-centered social creatures. They excel at being a member of a group. Many are also comfortable as mediators.

By contrast, as a group, firstborn children often display a strong need to achieve, and many seek power and authority. They tend to act like adults. Some take that a step further and act like self-appointed "bosses." They may even be viewed by younger siblings as oppressors. Last-born children tend to go their own way, to avoid "choosing up sides," and to be able to ignore admonitions or threats from those in power.

The typical high school student body in 2000 included a larger proportion of firstborns and of last-borns than was the pattern in the early 1970s. The proportion of middle-born students dropped by over half as a result of smaller families. One consequence was to create an environment that became more supportive of conflict.

The End of Monopolies

The most highly visible of these changes can be seen in the delivery of mail. While the United States Postal Service retains its monopoly on the delivery of conventional first-class letters, it is now faced with mounting competition (see chapter 8). For decades the American Telephone and Telegraph Company enjoyed a monopoly on long-distance telephone services. By 1999 AT&T had 300 competitors. Monopolies served America well up through the first half of the twentieth century.

The deregulation of the trucking industry and the airlines in the 1980s brought greater competition to those slices of the transportation world. Likewise, automobiles manufactured by corporations in Germany, Japan, and Korea have transformed that industry in the United States. As recently as the 1950s the small family farm competed with other small family farms. Now the small labor-intensive American farm is competing with the large capital-intensive farm as well as with imports from other countries. The retail stores on Main Street must compete with the shopping centers and the discount stores.

Competition is the deadly enemy of monopolies.

The Consumer-driven Marketplace

A fifth trend that is relevant to this discussion can be summarized by what many see as a dirty word. That word is *consumerism*. Today's consumers demand relevance, quality, choice, and convenience. That helps to explain why so many small hospitals have closed. That helps to explain why the large shopping center has replaced Main Street. That helps to explain the gradual disappearance of the physician in solo practice. That helps to explain the replacement of the small neighborhood congregation by the large regional church. That helps to explain the increase in the number of children being home schooled by parents. That helps to explain the changes in the size, shape, design, and cost of private motor vehicles. That also explains why so many very large and expensive sports stadiums constructed in the 1950–80 era have been replaced in recent years.

The perspective, control, value system, and convenience of the producers are being undermined by the demands of the consumer. One size no longer fits all.

The Consequences of Affluence

In the 1930s a wristwatch was a common reward for graduation from high school. In the 1990s the gift of an automobile was the highlight in the celebration of a sixteenth birthday.

The rising level of affluence in American society plus the widening gap between those at the top of the economic ladder and those at the bottom plus the growth of egalitarianism have combined to create pressures for greater equality of opportunity. One road to equality is through better-quality education for the children of the poor and the children of ethnic minority groups. Education has become one facet of the civil rights movement.

One product of the discontent with the current system of public education is a growing demand for tax-funded vouchers to enable children from at-risk home environments to attend a school of their choice.

Choice once was a key word in the national debate over abortion. It now is a key word in the struggle for racial and ethnic equality in education.

The Electronic Era

The newest and perhaps the most influential of all these trends is the arrival of the electronic era. A simple illustration is that the videotape is supplementing the teacher/student relationship in the classroom. The most profound example is the arrival of the Internet.

Distance learning is now being experienced largely by people born before 1985, but it soon will be commonplace among those born after 1995. Distance learning already is becoming a vital resource for home schoolers.

The Evolution of the American Public High School

The walk to the schoolhouse door was replaced by the school bus with a surveillance camera.

The walk to school by a group of children that often evolved into a meaningful social network, the school bus, the schoolhouse, and face-to-face interaction are now being replaced by the web site, the Internet, and the online high school.

Technology is the new enemy of the old monopolies.

Better-educated Parents

As recently as 1940 one-half of the adults in the American population had less than an eighth-grade education. The high school teacher or principal who had completed four years of college or university training obviously was in a better position to determine what would be a good learning environment for a teenager than was the parent who had never been to high school or had dropped out after a year or two.

Today it is not unusual for a parent with two or three or more years of post-graduate education to conclude that he or she is better educated than the high school teacher with only one year of post-graduate education. This new generation of well-educated parents constitutes a constituency different from the constituency of the 1940s or 1950s!

The Impact of Participatory Democracy

The radicals of the early 1960s proclaimed that every citizen had a right to participate in the decisions that would shape his or her future.[1] This "right" was a major factor in killing the Clinton proposal in 1993 to create a new system for delivering health-care services. This new affirmation of "interest-group democracy" precipitated the disruption of the meeting of the World Trade Organization in Seattle in November 1999.

The radical proposal of the early 1960s has become a widely accepted right thirty-five years later. Teachers and students now believe that they have a God-given right to shape the learning environment in their public high school. The counsel of the professional experts should be available, but the teacher and the students should be partners in determining which pieces of advice should be implemented and which should be ignored. Participatory democracy is transforming the roles of parents, principals, school board members, and educational experts as well as the roles of students and teachers.

The End of the Melting Pot?

For many generations the public school in the United States was widely perceived to be an essential component of a larger strategy for socializing children into a common culture. The rich and the poor studied side by side in the same room with the same teacher. The native-born and the recent immigrant child learned together and played together. The public school was a powerful force in the Americanization of the children from immigrant families.

The big exception, of course, was the racial segregation of the public schools. One of the most persuasive arguments in support of school busing was to create a colorblind America.

Among the most determined proponents of the public school as a means of assimilating "outsiders" into the mainstream of American society were Jewish parents.

The post-civil rights era of the 1980s and 1990s brought the emergence of a new ideological position. Ethnic pride and ethnic identity are crucial components of this new ideology. Ethnic separation began to rival ethnic integration. One facet of this was the demand for monocultural dormitories and departments of ethnic studies in colleges and universities. Another was the organization of ethnic caucuses in several predominantly Anglo religious bodies. A third was the demand for bilingual education in the public schools. A fourth was the establishment of quotas in employment, in college admissions, and in filling leadership positions. A fifth was the creation of all-black private elementary schools. A sixth was the opposition by many of the black clergy to efforts by Anglo denominations to "cream off" their upwardly mobile members to create new African American congregations in what was still a predominantly white denomination. A seventh was the organization of

Saturday schools for their children by immigrants from China. An eighth was the organization of new immigrant religious congregations. A ninth was the election of an ethnic leader by an ethnic constituency to city, state, and congressional offices. A tenth was to use ethnicity as an influential criterion in selecting people for high governmental offices.

The goal of a colorblind society was replaced by the demand for recognition and affirmation of ethnic identity.

One of the most widely overlooked, but highly symbolic, examples of this is the recent emergence of new Jewish schools. For more than a hundred years the public school was widely perceived by Jewish parents as an essential part of the strategy for Jews to be accepted as Americans.

During the last third of the twentieth century, however, the number of children enrolled in full-time Jewish schools more than tripled. The proportion of Jewish children enrolled in public schools dropped from over 90 percent in 1962 to approximately 65 percent in 1999.[2]

How does a religious movement transmit its faith, culture, and history to younger generations? How does a religious movement increase the probability that the children will marry someone from the same religious faith?

In the last half of the nineteenth century, the Roman Catholic Church in America concluded that the best answer to both questions was a network of parochial schools and Catholic colleges. Lutheran immigrants from Europe came to the same conclusion. Subsequently, Seventh Day Adventists created their own educational network to maintain and perpetuate their distinctive identity. Today more than a score of historically black colleges continue to exist as part of a larger strategy of reinforcing racial identity and self-expression.

For more than a century a central part of the ideological foundation for the tax-supported public school was the goal of ethnic integration. Today one of the central ideological arguments for subsidizing the consumer, rather than the producer, of educational services is to strengthen the racial, ethnic, religious, and nationality self-identities of children and youth.

What Day Is It?

Privatization and Outsourcing

A rapidly growing number of municipalities have decided to contract with private for-profit companies for the collection of garbage, the design of a new highway, the inservice training experiences for employees, the reassessment of real estate for tax purposes, the operation of a paramedic-staffed ambulance service, the advice of legal counsel, or a national search for a new department head.

Likewise, many public school systems have decided to contract with private corporations for the education of students with severe emotional problems or major physical handicaps or who are prone to extreme expressions of antisocial behavior. Private consultants are now being hired by public school districts to provide guidance counseling for high school students in career planning and in preparing their applications for admissions to colleges and universities.[3]

The contemporary public school district often serves as the conduit for dollars gathered from taxpayers to be sent to the corporation that provides the educational services.

More recently in some states the school system collects the tax dollars that are either funneled into vouchers for students to attend a private school of their choice or to provide a per student payment to charter schools.

What is the future of the public school systems in the United States? To provide educational services for children and youth? Or to serve as a conduit for tax funds that will be sent to those corporations that provide the educational services? If the choice is to serve as a conduit, which will be the politically acceptable conduit in the twenty-first century? The local school district? Public universities? The state department of education? Or the United States Department of Education?

While far from an exhaustive list, these eleven changes have created a new context for discussing the future of tax-supported education in the new millennium.

When taken together, these eleven changes also raise new questions: Has the time come to reform the large public high school? Or is it too late? Has the time come to examine other alternatives to reform? An instructive model is to look briefly at what has happened to the United States postal system.

125

Chapter Eight

WHAT HAPPENED TO THE POST OFFICE?

F irst, they took our post office, and now they want to take our school!"

That cry of despair was heard in thousands of small towns across the United States during the twentieth century. The advocates of public school consolidation in the middle of the twentieth century persuaded state legislatures to provide financial incentives for the merging of small public school districts. The number of public schools (all grades) shrank from 262,236 in 1930 to 117,637 in 1960 to 86,000 in 1998. The number of public secondary schools held steady at approximately 25,000, while the enrollment nearly quadrupled between 1930 and 2000.

The public school, the general store, and the post office had been important components of the distinctive identity of that small town. That earlier decision to close the post office had been followed several years later by the failure to find a buyer when the owner of the general store died. The recent rumor that the school would be closed sounded like a death knell for this community.

Back in the 1960s city planners agreed that revival of the economically deteriorating central business district required retention of a downtown location for the city hall, the county courthouse, at least a couple of financial institutions, one or two motion picture theaters, at least one department store, the main post office, the public library, and other attractions for pedestrian traffic.

The United States Post Office originated as a government-owned and operated monopoly for the delivery of mail. It was mandated in Section 8, Article I of the United States Constitution, which was ratified in 1789.

Thanks to such innovations as paved roads, canals, railroads, gasoline-powered motor vehicles, and the airplane, that monopoly served the country well for nearly two centuries.

An important symbol reinforcing the identity of a new community was the arrival of its own post office. The number of post offices in the United States increased from 8,450 in 1830 to 28,492 in 1870 and then jumped to 42,989 in 1880. That number peaked at 76,945 in 1901. In 1927, for the first time since 1884, it dropped below 50,000 and stood at only 28,189 (exclusive of 10,000 branches) in 1996.

In addition to facilitating the delivery of the mail, those 50,000 to 77,000 post offices offered several fringe benefits: (1) The local post office was a convenient and heavily used place for residents to meet and exchange local gossip. (2) The system provided tens of thousands of steady indoor and well-paying jobs for adults. (3) The existence of a post office constituted a symbol declaring that this is a viable and important community. (4) The system connected the residents of a huge and growing nation, thus reinforcing a sense of national unity. (5) It provided useful patronage for politicians. And (6) with the creation of rural-free delivery and the parcel post service, farmers and small-town residents gained easy access to a new retail world called the mail-order catalog—a virtual department store delivered to the mailbox.

In recent decades what once was a government-owned monopoly has had to adjust to competition in the form of the telegraph, the telephone, radio, television, fax machines, the United Parcel Service, Federal Express, e-mail, e-commerce, and cost-benefit ratios. One consequence was the creation of the United States Postal Service in 1970 to free the system from political pressures so it could become economically viable. A second was that the pressure of competition forced the introduction of overdue innovations.

Will the local post office, which continues as a central component of the distinctive identity for at least 20,000 small towns, survive through the early decades of the twenty-first century? One answer is that it depends on its capability to innovate and compete in a marketplace filled with an unprecedented level of competition. In 1999 nearly 30 percent of the gross revenues of the Postal Service came from the sending and paying of bills. By 2003 most of those bills and payments probably will be sent via the World Wide Web. One way to pay those current bills, and perhaps to reduce that accumulated deficit of $3.5 billion, is to issue a larger number and greater variety of commemorative stamps every year. Producing and selling "collectibles" has become a new core purpose of both the Postal Service and the United States Treasury Department.

Will the Postal Service be able to survive that new level of competition?

A second answer to that question is that this is a big concern (a) for 800,000 employees of the Postal Service and (b) for millions of people born in the 1920–60 era. A third answer is that relatively few Americans born after 1970 care. They are more concerned about easy access to reliable, effective, and economic channels of communication. They are less concerned about the institutional survival of government-owned monopolies created by white males who have been dead for many decades.

A parallel trend can be seen in the number and location of motion picture threaters. As recently as the 1950s they, along with several historic tall-steeple churches with a non-geographically defined constituency, were essential components of the downtown business district. Today nearly all the multiplex movie theaters and the Protestant megachurches are located in suburbia. The number of such theaters in the United States dropped from 20,843 in 1954 to 6,700 in 1998.

A plentiful supply of well-educated workers, a convention center, perhaps a major-league sports stadium, an interactive children's museum, and an array of restaurants, hotels, and specialty retail shops have moved ahead of the post office, motion picture theaters, department stores, First Church downtown, and the grocery store in revitalizing the central business district.

What Happened to the Post Office?

What Is the Issue?

Which is the higher priority? Providing Americans with faster, easier, cheaper, better, and a greater variety of systems for the transmission of messages and the delivery of packages? Or perpetuating a government-owned monopoly that reinforces the distinctive identity of a community as a place on the map?[1]

How will the people born in the 1920s vote on that question? How will the people born after 1970 vote on that question? Which of those two generations will have the greater influence in the twenty-first century?

A parallel question concerns the role of the tax-supported public high school. Why does it exist? To provide a sense of identity for a community? To attract enough gifted athletes to win the state championship in football or basketball? To help perpetuate a government-mandated monopoly? Or to challenge contemporary teenagers with a variety of customized learning communities that are designed to enable them to fulfill their potential?

What Is the Answer?

In the contemporary American culture, the future of both sets of government-managed monopolies will not be determined by tradition. The future of the United States Postal Service and of the tax-supported public high school will be determined by how effective they are in adapting to a far more competitive culture than existed in 1960. Relevant responses to the increasingly diverse agendas of the constituency plus innovative and customized services have moved ahead of tradition in determining the future of government-owned and operated monopolies!

The Postal Service must decide what it does best and not attempt to compete in those functions where it is weak. That raises a relevant question: What do the large public high schools do best? That answer, however, must be postponed until chapter 10.

The Evolution of the American Public High School

The *Big* Trade Off

The post office serving 40,000 residents is a far different ecological environment from the one serving 300 residents. A trip
to the small-town post office often was an enjoyable experience.
That visit usually included an encounter with a postal clerk
who was a friend, possibly a neighbor, and perhaps even a political crony. The patron often was greeted by name. That visit
usually included a few minutes of conversation with one or
more friends who happened to be present at that moment.

Today's trip to that large regional post office may mean
standing in line with strangers and transacting one's business at
the counter with a total stranger. What once was a pleasureable
experience has become a chore. It is easier to have United
Parcel Service pick up that package rather than to make a trip
to the post office.

The neighborhood movie theater used to be a place for a family
outing. Frequently that visit carried the bonus of a brief conversation with friends and acquaintances. The new multiplex is
an entertainment center subsidized by the sale of refreshments.
Cable television and videotapes have become the entertainment equivalent of home schooling in education just as e-mail
is replacing the family letter sent by "snail mail."

The congregation of that small neighborhood church was
glued together by kinship ties, neighborliness, a strong denominational loyalty, local traditions, a shared religious commitment, and a variety of other relationships. The regional
megachurch attracts and holds people primarily through its passion for relevance and quality and its capability to offer people
a broad range of meaningful choices in worship, learning, vol-
unteering in ministry, fellowship, and personal spiritual
growth.

Function, efficiency, quality, and choice have moved ahead of
relationships.

To be more specific, the professionals won the battle to
reduce the number of post offices, but the price tag on that victory was an erosion of that broad-based public support for the

130

What Happened to the Post Office?

Postal Service. E-commerce is not producing a great surge in the volume of packages shipped via the Postal Service. Grandma does not feel guilty about using e-mail to communicate with the children and grandchildren rather than relying on snail mail.

Likewise, the professional educators won the school consolidation battle. They also won the battle for increased state and federal aid to local school districts. The price tags on those victories, however, include apathy, alienation, adversarial relationships between parents and school officials, adversarial relationships between the teachers and the school administrators, and, most of all, an erosion of trust.

The four-year public high school with 100 to 200 students, largely financed by direct taxes on local residents, was designed to foster local support. Most of the parents were personally acquainted with every member of the school board and with most of the teachers. It was organized around relationships and trust.

The contemporary four-year public high school with an enrollment of 1,200 students is organized around anonymity, complexity, state and federally mandated goals, interscholastic athletic competition, a bureaucratic structure, and a minimal level of parental involvement.

The old system produced questions from parents such as these: "When do we meet the new teacher?" "How can we help?" "What can I do to help my son do better in school?" "What can we do to help pass that school bond issue?" "Who should we ask to become the next PTA president?"

The new system often evokes a different set of questions: "Are we getting our fair share of state aid?" "Why is the school bus late so often?" "Aren't the teachers too quick to recommend psychotropic drugs?" "Why was my kid expelled?" "School taxes already are too high! You're telling me they want to increase the school levy?" "Are we getting our share of federal aid?" "Why are the test scores in our school so low?" "Why are the administrators getting such high salaries while our classroom teachers are underpaid?" "Do we really need that many administrators?" "Why do the high school classes have to begin so early every morning?"

The Evolution of the American Public High School

Five guiding generalizations are useful in reflecting on the consequences of these victories in school consolidation and financing. First, an effective way to increase alienation is to ask people to send their tax dollars to a distant place where strangers will decide the final destination of those dollars. Second, the greater the degree of anonymity and complexity that are built into a system, the lesser the satisfaction the consumers receive from relationships. That satisfaction from relationships is replaced by higher expectations for quality, a high level of performance, and clear accountability. Third, the greater the emphasis on a centralized command-and-control organizational structure, the easier it is for the constituents to patronize a competitor.

Fourth, it is impossible to translate these issues into traditional "liberal" and "conservative" categories.[2] The civil rights movement, for example, is divided over the merits and costs of school busing and vouchers.[3]

Finally, the larger, the more complex, and the more anonymous the system and the younger the constituency, the more likely the constituent's number-one criterion in evaluation will not be, "How is our organization doing?" Rather, it will be, "Are my needs being met?" If the answer is in the negative, it is easy to shop a competitor.

United Parcel Service, Federal Express, e-commerce, cable television, the 120,000-square-foot supermarket, the mail-order pharmacy, home schooling, videotape sales, the regional megachurch, and charter schools are among the contemporary responses to those negative evaluations by consumers.

Those victories also have evoked a series of public-policy questions, but that requires another chapter.

Chapter Nine

TEN PUBLIC POLICY QUESTIONS

The number of Americans who are dissatisfied with the public school system in the United States is increasing. Few will deny that is a fact of contemporary reality. The big debate is over what can be done about the current state of affairs. What is the best beginning point? Enlist better people in a teaching career? Reform teacher-training programs? Raise the compensation for classroom teachers? Reduce class size? Increase the budget of the United States Department of Education? Test all teachers on the subject matter they teach? Improve inservice training for teachers? Recruit better principals? Encourage Congress to adopt national standards? Require more post-graduate education of teachers? Construct new school buildings? Raise taxes? Create safer schools?

That list could be expanded to at least a hundred suggestions.

A more useful beginning point may be to look at the larger context in the form of public-policy questions. Ten of these stand out, from this observer's perspective.

1. WHICH ADULTS CAN BE TRUSTED?

In early 1946, twenty-three-year-old Sergeant John Smith was discharged from the United States Army. Thanks to the tax-subsidized G.I. Bill of Rights of 1944, he was able to enroll in the college or university of his choice. The assumption was that he could be trusted to make a wise choice on how to spend that tax-subsidized voucher for his tuition as well as that monthly check for housing and meals.

Several years later, he and his wife, Mary, purchased a single-family home with a twenty-year mortgage. Every March, when they filed their federal income tax, John and Mary enjoyed a federally subsidized benefit as they deducted the previous year's general property tax and interest payments from their gross income in calculating their taxable income. The federal government did not restrict their choice of place of residence in granting that subsidy. The government trusted John and Mary to make that decision on where they wanted to live.

John and Mary contributed generously to religious and charitable organizations. Those contributions also were partially subsidized by the United States government.

When their three children were ready for school, however, the local government offered them two choices. Their children could be enrolled in a heavily tax-subsidized public elementary school down the street. "Since we do not trust you, John and Mary, that is a 'take it or leave it' choice. Your other option is to enroll your children in private schools, and you pay the cost."

In essence, the message was, "When you were young and single, John, we, your government, trusted you to make wise use of that tax-funded voucher. Today, however, you are past thirty, married, and a parent, and we do not believe you can be trusted to make wise choices for your children. This is a free country, however, so if you're willing to pay the bill, you may enroll your children in any school of your choice; but we won't subsidize your choice. We will subsidize our choice for your children, but not yours."

The decades rolled by, and in 1988 World War II veteran John Smith celebrated his sixty-fifth birthday.

One option might have been this message from the United States government: "Congratulations, John! You have earned the right to a leisurely retirement. You have not, however, earned the trust of your government. We have just completed construction of a new retirement community in northern Arizona. You and Mary may move into a new apartment there, and we, your friends in Washington, will pay all the costs for rent, utilities, meals, and local taxes for as long as you and Mary care to live there."

A second message might have been, "John, you're getting old, and you're wearing out. You and Mary will need far more medical care over the next several years than you have needed before you retired. In addition to free housing, we will provide you with the care of a physician of our choice and, if needed, hospital care, in that retirement community in the Sunbelt. At your age, John, we do not believe we can trust you to select your own physician and your own hospital, so we have assigned you to a primary-care physician of our choice as well as to a hospital of our choice."

With the exception of those who turned to the Veterans Administration for help, those two messages were neither sent nor received. Instead, John received this message: "When you were discharged from military service, we trusted you to make wise educational decisions. We also trusted you to make a wise investment when you and Mary purchased that house, and we helped subsidize your mortgage payments for twenty years. We also trusted you to be a good steward when you contributed your money to charitable and religious causes, and we partially subsidized those contributions.

"It was not until your first child was ready for kindergarten that we, your government, began to distrust your judgment. It was clear to us that you and Mary could not be trusted to decide where the tax subsidy for your children's education should be directed. Therefore, we made that choice for you.

"Now that you're sixty-five, John, we have concluded that you are sufficiently mature to make wise decisions on such matters as your housing, your diet, your travel, and your health care. Therefore, we have enrolled you in Social Security and Medicare. We are convinced that you can be trusted to decide where you want to live and to choose your own doctor and hospital. You can count on the United States Treasury to mail you a tax-funded Social Security check every month and on Medicare to pay most of your health-care costs. Now that you and Mary are empty nesters, you have earned the trust we had in you before you became parents."

Should the current public policy that declares that nineteen- and twenty-three-year-old university students and mature adults in their late sixties can be trusted, while the thirty-one-year-old parent cannot be trusted, become permanent public policy?

One response is that John "earned" that voucher by serving in World War II. Subsequently, John and Mary both contributed to Social Security and Medicare, so they have earned a right to a return on their taxes. John's reply was, "While our children were in school, we paid both property and income taxes to support the education of children, but we were told we could not be trusted to choose the school."

Should age and/or marital status be central criteria in determining which adults can be trusted?

2. WHAT ARE FAIR EXPECTATIONS?

Systems produce what they are designed to produce.

An effective strategy for producing failure in an institution or organization includes seven components: (1) The projected expectations exceed what that system was designed to produce. (2) The current resources are inadequate for meeting those expectations. (3) There is an absence of widespread agreement on the primary purpose for the continued existence of that organization. (4) There is an absence of widespread agreement on the primary constituency for that organization. (5) The people working in that organization are not prepared or equipped to fulfill many of the expectations projected of that organization. (6) There is an absence of agreement on the criteria to be used in evaluating that organization. (7) The potential for creativity and innovation is restricted by externally generated rules, regulations, and unfunded mandates.

That summarizes why the large American public high school is designed for failure. It also explains why teachers are set up to fail. (For more on that point, see chapter 12.)

One extravagant expectation is that the public school is expected to function as a healthy surrogate family constellation for youngsters coming from dysfunctional home environments.

136

Another is that the school is expected to diagnose and treat the problems of emotionally troubled or psychologically unhealthy pupils and other concerns.

A third is that the public high school is expected to graduate emotionally healthy and self-directed teenagers who are motivated by the joy of learning.

A fourth is that the large public high school is expected to serve as a farm club for university athletic teams.

A fifth is the expectation that the public high school will nurture and develop the "whole person." That transfers to the high school a responsibility traditionally placed on the family, the community, the religion, the workplace, and the person's social network.

A sixth is the expectation that the high school will challenge all students to fulfill their potential as individuals and as contributing citizens in a democratic society.

Are those reasonable expectations to place on the teachers and administrators in a large public high school?

The history of secondary education, and to a lesser degree of institutions of higher education in America, is that, yes, those are reasonable expectations to project of *residential* high schools and of *residential* colleges. The four tax-supported national military academies are examples of how this long list of expectations can be placed on a residential school. Hundreds of residential high schools, both private and tax-supported, offer other examples.

This introduces a four-way fork in the public-policy road. Should the expectations of the large public high school be more narrowly focused to be compatible with reality? Or should taxpayers be asked to fund several thousand residential secondary schools that can be designed to fulfill that huge range of expectations? Or should the system be reformed around the creation of challenging learning communities (see chapter 12)? Or should we continue to set teachers and students up to fail?

3. WHAT DO WE EXPECT OF PARENTS?

The tradition in the American economy has called for parents to accept the responsibility for sheltering, clothing, and feeding their children. During the past several decades a variety of systems of financial subsidies has been designed and provided to parents who are unable to meet all three of those responsibilities. One is public housing. That system was designed to use tax funds to house low-income families. The tax-funded financial subsidy went directly to the provider of the service. It is difficult today to find people who will evaluate public housing as a success story. There are exceptions! At least two dozen subsidized public housing ventures now accommodate professionals with a family income in the $60,000 to $90,000 range.

This introduces the third of these public-policy questions: Who should pay for the education of today's youth and children? The current answer is, "Taxes should be used to pay those costs if the students enroll in public schools, but the parents should pay if the children attend a private school or are taught at home by parents." That generalization is riddled with a growing number of exceptions. On one side, the fees charged high school students continue to climb. On the other side, the number of tax-financed subsidies for students in private schools continues to increase. In several geographically defined public school districts, one-fifth to one-third of all federal dollars sent to schools in that community are directed to private schools for textbooks, transportation, equipment, staff, compensation, and other purposes.

The "fairness" argument contends that the number-one beneficiary of formal education is not the parents, but the nation as a whole. Therefore, tax dollars should be directed to finance all forms of education for children and youth.

During the 1998–99 school year more than one-third of the 180,000 students enrolled in the public schools in Detroit were absent at least 10 percent of the time. Does the responsibility for the regular attendance of students rest with the parents? Or with that local school district? Or with the police and judicial system?

Is it realistic to expect parents to obey compulsory attendance laws? Should parents be fined or sent to jail if they fail that assignment? An increasing number of parents, teenagers, and civil libertarians have concluded that it is unfair to hold one person responsible for the behavior of someone else. Should the driver's license of a truant be suspended for unexcused absences? Or should the compulsory attendance laws be repealed because they are unenforceable?

Rearing a rebellious two-year-old can be a challenging assignment. Hundreds of public school districts now offer tax-subsidized training programs for new parents. Should parenting classes also be offered for those rearing fourteen-year-olds?

A common public policy today is to require a license to marry, a license to drive a motor vehicle, a license to teach, and a license to practice law. Should a license be required of everyone who expects to become a parent? Or should a parenting license be required to bring a baby home from the hospital? Or to enroll a child in a public school? Which requires the highest level of commitment and skill? Constructing a two-car garage at the rear of a residential lot? Or rearing a teenager? Or driving a motor vehicle?

What are reasonable expectations to project of every parent?[1]

The safe assumption is that no one system will work perfectly in every situation. That means creating a backup system. While a spare tire is rarely needed today, most new automobiles come equipped with one.

If fewer than 100 percent of all parents will obey the compulsory attendance laws, what could be an effective backup system? If fewer than 100 percent of all parents are competent to rear children, what should be the backup system? One alternative is adoption. Another is foster-home care. Both, however, are more effective with young children than with teenagers.

If the combination of biological parents, blended families, single-parent homes, grandparents, adoptions, and foster care provided a satisfactory home environment for 99 percent of the nearly 70 million children and youth in America ages birth to seventeen, what about the other one percent? One possibility could be residential schools. What would be the annual operating cost for 700,000 children and youth in boarding schools? A modest estimate of $30,000 per person comes to $21 billion annually.

Who should be asked to pay the annual operating costs of a network of residential schools? The parents? The local school districts? Private philanthropists? Religious organizations? State governments? The federal government? Affluent grandparents?

Would that be a prudent investment of tax dollars? Or would it be better public policy to postpone those expenditures for later intervention through (a) expanded public-assistance programs, (b) job-training classes for illiterate adults, (c) more prisons, (d) substance abuse treatment centers, and (e) homes for dependent adults?

Finally, the recent demands that high school seniors pass a competency test before being granted a high school diploma have created a divisive issue. Should parents be expected to demand, or at least support, proposals for raising the academic bar for graduation from high school? Or should those responsible for defining standards expect that the majority of parents will favor "dumbing down" the curriculum and lowering the standards in order to increase the graduation rate?

What should be expected of parents in twenty-first-century America?

4. WHO WILL BE SUBSIDIZED?

Another high-priority public-policy issue is whether tax-financed subsidies should be directed to the producer or to the consumer of public subsidies. The dominant trend in the United States over the past seven decades, as described in chapter 7, has been in the direction of focusing more on subsidies for the consumers, rather than the institutions that produce those services.

The obviously attractive political response to that delicate either/or question is, "We'll subsidize both. We now use tax dollars to subsidize both the producers and the consumers of certain agricultural products, of health care, of military hardware, of higher education, of fire protection services, of professional baseball and football games, of public transportation, and of many other goods and services. Why make an exception for the education of children and youth?"

An important, but largely overlooked, trend in recent years has been for both the federal and state governments to focus on outcomes rather than inputs and to subsidize corporations to implement governmental goals. One example is the reliance on nongovernmental organizations (NGOs) for humanitarian relief on other continents.[2] A second is the use of private profit-driven corporations to implement the welfare-to-work programs.[3] A third is the use of tax funds for tuition for students attending profit-driven post-secondary schools.[4] A fourth is the use of tax dollars to fund private schools for children whom the public schools are unable or unwilling to accept.

In economic terms, the largest financial subsidy by the federal government during the twentieth century for the socialization and education of children and youth has been the free use of the nation's airwaves by radio and television stations. Another, much smaller but more direct financial subsidy has been to the Public Broadcasting System.

These public-policy decisions have many precedents. One was the subsidies for the construction of canals. Another was the land grants to wealthy corporations to build railroads across the west. A more recent public policy was to pay financially needy mothers to stay home and care for their children. That has been transformed in recent years to make it financially attractive for single-parent mothers to place their dependent children in child-care centers while the mothers are trained to participate in the labor market.

In recent years states and units of local government have offered huge financial subsidies out of tax dollars to prospective employers who promise to create new jobs for residents. In Canada, the prospective immigrant is welcomed who can promise to bring the money required to create new jobs.

The Illinois Math and Science Academy was created in 1985. It is a tax-supported, three-year residential high school with high admission standards and an enrollment of approximately 660 teenagers. Approximately 3 percent of all public school students in Illinois are of Asian ancestry and 13 percent are Latino. In 1998–99, 27 percent of the students enrolled in the Academy were Asian Americans, and 6 percent were Latino. Is the public-policy goal to provide an expensive and heavily subsidized high-quality educational experience for teenagers with an Asian ancestry?

A huge and persuasive body of research supports the contention that parents are by far the most influential teachers during a child's formative years.

Parents are by far the most influential teachers during a child's formative years.

Critics contend that, on balance, television is a negative influence in the socialization and education of children and youth.

This raises a crucial public-policy question: Would it be more consistent with national goals, which currently place a high value on the education of children and youth, to reduce that federal subsidy to television and financially encourage parents to school their children at home? Should the federal government tax the use of the nation's airwaves by television and radio stations and use those revenues to encourage and equip parents to be more effective teachers?

For the past two centuries the direction of public policy in the United States has been to subsidize the institutions that provide services. That long list includes mass transit, hospitals, long-distance trucking companies, public school systems, radio and television stations, corporate farms, private schools, cruise companies operating under a foreign flag, cemeteries, religious organizations, and mailorder catalog houses.

Has the time come to reconsider that tradition?

One alternative would be to begin by seeking agreement on a series of national goals. After that has been achieved, the hundreds of billions of dollars in financial subsidies could be awarded to those who are prepared to help attain those goals.

Another alternative, which has been the guiding principle in subsidizing a better life for the elderly, would be direct subsidies to the consumers of the services designed to attain that national goal.

That leads this discussion into a fifth public-policy issue.

5. WHAT SHOULD TAXES SUBSIDIZE?

Should tax dollars be used to perpetuate the old or to encourage creation of the new? One of the big examples on the federal level is the use of huge financial subsidies to encourage innovation in capital-intensive agriculture and also to encourage perpetuating the traditional, labor-intensive style of farming.

A second expensive example from the federal budget has been the decision to subsidize the creation of new weapons systems and resources for national defense while continuing to subsidize the operation of redundant military bases and the production of obsolete weapons of war.

A third example from this federal budget may be the most delicate political question: Should the United States government borrow money to subsidize the retirement and health care of needy adults? Or of both needy and financially comfortable adults? The answer, of course, has been both.

In dollar terms, the most important facet of this policy question on what taxes should subsidize can be stated very simply: Should tax dollars be used to subsidize failure or success? Incompetence or competence?

During the past two decades the messages received from the federal government have communicated a priority on subsidizing incompetence and failure. The 1999 failures of two space vehicles constitute only one example of subsidizing failure.

One of the most costly examples was the message received by federally insured savings and loan associations. "While this may not make economic sense to you, the federal government is prepared to subsidize any losses incurred when you pay a high rate of interest on deposits and loan money out at a lower interest rate and/or when you make unsound investments in real estate."

Another message was received by owners of residences on the Atlantic coast. "If your home was destroyed by a hurricane, the federal government will subsidize the rebuilding of your home and also subsidize your flood insurance premiums."

Many farmers received this message: "Here is a list of crops in which production usually exceeds market demand. If you plant one or more of the crops on the list, and the supply exceeds the market demand for that crop, the federal government will subsidize your operation."

Other farmers received this message: "Not only will we cover part of the losses you experienced when you planted crops in a flood plain, but we will also subsidize your efforts if you decide to continue to farm in that flood plain."

Those four messages have produced over $300 billion in federal subsidies during the past quarter century.

Since the enactment of Title I in federal education policy in 1965, two messages have been received.

"If your public school includes large numbers of poor and educationally deprived children, we will send you money every year. Whether you succeed or fail in your efforts to educate these children will not affect your subsidies. All we ask is that you continue to enroll them."

A completely different message was received by the Roman Catholic private schools in many of these same communities: "We admire your commitment to these poor and educationally deprived children. We admire your success in transforming the lives of many of these children, but because we are committed to subsidizing public institutions only, we cannot reward success in private schools."

By 1999, after spending $120 billion on Title I programs, a few members of the United States Congress were sufficiently bold to suggest that performance, not simply enrollment, should become a criterion for deciding what should be subsidized. Other members of Congress contended that Title I funds should be made available to a larger number of public schools.

The big risk for the public schools in this public-policy debate is that if success becomes a criterion for the awarding of federal funds to education, that could open the door to greater competition and to federal aid to private schools. That door already has been opened to private, profit-driven corporations in agriculture, public assistance, overseas humanitarian relief efforts, the design of space vehicles, finance,

144

transportation, manufacturing, and logging. Why not in education?

> **The big risk for the public schools in this public-policy debate is that if success becomes a criterion for the awarding of federal funds to education, that could open the door to greater competition and to federal aid to private schools.**

Given these and thousands of other politically attractive "both-and" responses to those "either-or" questions about the allocation of scarce tax dollars, is it reasonable to hope that public funds could be used to perpetuate the traditional public high school and also to subsidize the creation of new learning centers?

Does the fact that the large public high school, designed to fill the role of a warehouse or a factory or a prison, often cannot compete with the private Roman Catholic or Lutheran high school or with a new charter school justify cutting off the financial subsidy to that public school?

The United States has a long history of using tax dollars to subsidize both failure and success, so this is not a new public-policy issue! The real issue is, Why stop now?

6. WHAT IS THE NUMBER-ONE GOAL OF GRANTING THESE FINANCIAL SUBSIDIES?

A frequently articulated goal is to "save the public schools." That is consistent with the American political tradition that calls for subsidizing failure and for perpetuating obsolete institutions.

Should that tradition drive public-policy formulation in the twenty-first century? Or should the new national public policy be to prepare and equip adolescents to become healthy, happy, contributing, and self-reliant citizens in a pluralistic democratic society?

7. DO WE BELIEVE EVERY CHILD CAN EXCEL?

Those who give a high priority to making this a better world for children will argue that this question belongs at the top of the agenda. They are right! It does. The sequence used here is process driven and is not designed to reflect the importance of the issues.

This question calls for resurrecting an old cliché and transforming it into an attainable goal. The old cliché was that every child can learn. That is a noble dream! A modest operational goal would be that every young person can and should be challenged to learn how to excel in at least one aspect of life in the American culture. If a youngster learns how to excel once, it is relatively easy to learn something else. Success builds self-confidence. More important, learning how to succeed proves, "I can learn. I'm not a dummy!"

This is the number-one reason why schools should offer instruction in golf, shop, mathematics, the English language, history, sewing, reading, writing, tennis, computer sciences, karate, public speaking, basketball, welding, photography, music, art, skiing, and other opportunities for individual excellence.

A passing grade of C will be earned by students who can authentically boast, "I can do that better than either of my parents or any of my siblings" (excellence within one's family constellation). A grade of B for superior performance will be awarded the student who is able to declare, "I can do that better than any of my friends can" (excellence within one's social network). A grade of A will be granted to the student who can proclaim, "I can do that better than anyone else in my class" (excellence among peers).

One alternative is to turn that responsibility over to the streets, where a few youngsters earn the right to boast, "I can jump start a car quicker than anyone I know." "I've impregnated more girls than anyone else in my gang." "I've been picked up by the cops more often than any kid in my neighborhood." "I'm a better shoplifter than anyone I've ever met."

Human beings have a need to learn how to excel. Who will meet that need for babies born in the 1990s?

Ten Public Policy Questions

The second half of this public-policy question is whether learning environments can and should be created to challenge every child and youth to learn to excel as a contributing member of a winning team.

If the larger societal goal includes preparing people to be contributing members of a team in the labor force or to enjoy a healthy, happy, and enduring marriage or to be a good neighbor or to become an active participant in the American political process or to become an effective high school teacher, this emphasis on enabling youngsters to excel as a team member also should be given a high priority.

This emphasis also explains why high schools should be organized as a collection of teams, rather than as a loose gathering of individuals. It also helps to explain why a high school should encourage students to participate in a marching band or play on a soccer team or become a member of the school orchestra or play football or be a member of the editorial staff of the school newspaper or help produce videotapes or join the school choir or be a member of a debate team or participate in competitive rowing or join a drama group or enroll in a class organized as a collection of teams rather than as a collection of individuals.

An attainable goal would be that forty-five months after enrolling in ninth grade every student would have earned three certificates. One would be a high school diploma. A second would declare that the student has achieved a level of excellence in one area of individual performance. The third would certify that the student has earned an award of excellence as a member of a team.

Forty-five months after enrolling in ninth grade every student would have earned three certificates. One, a diploma. Second, a level of excellence in one area of individual performance. Third, an award of excellence as a member of a team.

147

8. SHOULD GOVERNMENTAL MANDATES FOCUS ON INPUTS OR OUTCOMES?

This is one of the hotly debated contemporary public-policy questions: What will be the most productive points of intervention by government?

The traditional policy is that government should intervene on the input side. That includes minimum standards for being awarded a certificate to teach in that state, pensions and other compensation for teachers, the design of school buildings, criteria for participation in interscholastic athletics, requisite courses for graduation, educational requirements for principals and superintendents, minimum expenditures per students, maximum class size, minimum number of days in a school year to be eligible for state aid, criteria for tax-supported transportation for students, and dozens of other standards.

The standard complaint is that a student can graduate from a high school that meets all these mandates, but still not be able to read the diploma awarded at graduation.

In recent years a rising tide of interest has emerged to demand higher standards for graduation. These are based on two assumptions: The student is the number-one client of the high school, and it is reasonable to expect those four years to be a productive learning experience for every student.

The recent surge of interest in testing tenth- and twelfth-graders on what they have learned represents this new emphasis on outcomes. But that demand can motivate a "Teach to the test" pedagogical style.

One guiding generalization on this public-policy issue is that it is far easier to introduce new standards and new criteria for evaluation in a new institution than it is to replace the old criteria in an aging and tradition-driven institution.

A second guiding generalization is that it is easier to initiate litigation on ideological inputs rather than on outcomes.

One example of this is the current debate over whether federal funds should be allocated to wiring every private school into the World Wide Web. If addressed from the input side, this becomes an ideological debate over the use of tax dollars for private schools. Or should taxpaying parents pay for that out of their after-tax dollars?

If this issue is discussed from an outcome perspective, the question could be, "Was it a productive investment of federal funds after World War II to subsidize the education of veterans in private colleges and universities?" Or the issue could be stated in futuristic terms: "Is it in the national interest for every high school graduate to be computer literate?"

9. WOULD VOUCHERS ENHANCE RESPONSIBILITY?

Four of the most widely offered arguments in support of granting parents tax-funded vouchers for the education of their children are (1) to provide a wider range of choices, (2) to raise the level of accountability of the schools to the parents by the expansion of the educational marketplace,[5] (3) to level the playing field among the various types of schools, and (4) to place economic pressures on the "bad schools" to reform their philosophy and practices.

Monopolies do tend to generate passivity among consumers. If parents had to make a choice from among several schools, could the school accepting that voucher require parents to fulfill greater responsibilities in the education of their children? Could that moral contract include the parents' responsibility for making sure that student does attend school? For participation in parent/teacher consultations? For contributing X number of hours annually as a volunteer? For overseeing homework?

The current tax-funded subsidy to the producer of educational services does tend to encourage irresponsibility.

The message received by many parents suggests, "Our system offers a free education for your children. This means the school accepts the total responsibility for complying with state compulsory attendance laws requiring the daily attendance of your child. This also means that, if necessary, the school will accept the responsibility for providing your child with one or two nutritious free meals daily, possibly with clothing, and, in many cases, with free after-school care. The less you as a parent do for your child, the more this school will do to step in and fill the role of a surrogate parent."

One of the essential components of a strategy to build a high-performance organization is to project high expectations of all participants in that organization. Is it possible to build a high-performance, free public school by projecting low expectations of the parents—who often are the most influential teachers in that larger system?

Does the present system of subsidizing the producer of educational services set up the teacher, the student, and the parent for failure?

10. WHAT IS THE QUESTION?

The most ancient, and one of the most effective, organizing principles to transform a loose collection of individuals, clans, and factions into a closely knit, cohesive, and unified group is to identify a common enemy and organize against that enemy. It helps if that enemy can be personalized. Adolf Hitler used that organizing principle by identifying Jews as the enemy. In the early 1940s the United States used that principle in organizing the war effort. In recent years several dictators have identified the United States as the enemy as part of a larger strategy to continue in power.

Four great Protestant crusades have had an enormous impact on the United States. Each one has been organized around an identifiable enemy.

The first, and the most successful, was the Protestant crusade to create a nationwide system of tax-supported public "common schools" that would transmit an evangelical Protestant religious value system and cultural capital to the next generation. The common enemy for much of the history of this crusade from the 1820s through the 1950s was Roman Catholicism.

The second was the anti-slavery movement of the nineteenth century, which produced the Civil War, radical changes in the Constitution, and a new sense of a national identity. The common enemy was slavery.

The third movement was Prohibition, which produced two amendments to the Constitution. The common enemy was the alcoholic beverage.

The most recent was the civil rights movement. The common enemy was white racism and racial segregation.

Will efforts to create a better learning environment for children and youth in the twenty-first century be organized around identifying a common enemy? Or around offering attractive choices in learning environments that are compatible with a pluralistic and democratic society?

For more than a hundred years advocates of the tax-supported public "common school" in the United States used that ancient organizing principle to win support for their cause. In state after state, fear of Roman Catholicism was a powerful force in rallying support for the common school movement. The Protestant clergy were among the most highly visible, influential, articulate, and active supporters of the common school. The American Bible Society and the American Education Society (the successor to the American Society for Educating Pious Youth for the Christian Ministry) were incorporated in 1816. Each was the creation of evangelical Protestants.

In 1831 Alexis de Tocqueville commented on the influence of the Protestant clergy by noting that "almost all education is entrusted to them." Six decades later other scholars declared that the early public schools in New York and Massachusetts were largely the creations of Protestant clergy.

Protestant ministers were among the leaders in introducing the common school movement into the southern states in the second half of the nineteenth century, and several held the office of state superintendent of public schools. Protestant clergy wrote many of the textbooks used in the elementary schools of the nineteenth century. The Reverend William Holmes McGuffey was the most famous of these.[6]

In many state legislatures the political lobbying to secure state approval and financial support of the public common school was led by Protestant ministers. They usually made it clear that the Roman Catholic Church was the enemy in this battle.

The Evolution of the American Public High School

"Nonsectarian" education was defined as a public tax-supported school organized around an evangelical Protestant religious ethos in contrast to Catholic parochial schools. Methodists, Baptists, Presbyterians, and, to a lesser extent, Congregationalists were among the leaders in defining the public common school as an essentially Protestant institution. Textbooks in reading, history, and geography frequently carried anti-Catholic themes.

It was widely assumed that only three kinds of schools existed in the United States. The most numerous were tax-supported public evangelical Protestant schools. A distant second were Roman Catholic schools. In third place was that small number of user-funded private academies.

The battle line was drawn between the tax-supported public schools organized around a Protestant religious ethos and the Roman Catholic parochial schools.

The second half of the twentieth century was devoted to redrawing the battle lines. One line of demarcation placed all value-driven private schools on one side and all "value-free" public schools on the other side. Another redefined "nonsectarian" to include all public schools, while "sectarian" referred to religious schools. A third, and more recent, dividing line called for replacing the old anti-Catholic stance with a new rallying point calling for complete separation of the state from all Christian schools, both Catholic and Protestant.

More recently a new line of demarcation has been drawn to distinguish between "successful," or "good," schools and those identified as "failures," or "bad," schools. In searching for a new place of residence, one of the first questions asked by many parents is, "Is this a community with good schools?"

As emphasized in earlier chapters, however, the search for an enemy continues. Replacements for the Roman Catholic parochial school as the number-one enemy include gangs, television, motion pictures, affluence, the shopping mall, video games, secularism, alcohol, mothers employed outside the home, guns, drugs, cars, part-time jobs during the school year, disengaged parents, fundamentalists, teacher-training schools, principals, computers, lack of money, school busing, and a score of other potential villains.

Ten Public Policy Questions

An Instructive Parallel

Australia has had a parallel experience with public schools organized around a Protestant religious ethos. Their experience includes the emergence of a network of private Roman Catholic schools designed to perpetuate the Catholic religious faith and to transmit a distinctive cultural capital, plus a long political battle over the allocation of tax dollars to private schools. In Australia, unlike the United States, however, the issue has been identified in more positive terms.

For three decades the public policy discussions in Australia have emphasized five themes. One is the parents' right to choice in the education of their children. A second is how to live together in a pluralistic democracy. A third is the formulation of acceptable criteria for allocating governmental funds among public schools, private religious schools, and private nonsectarian schools. A fourth is the debate over whether a small democracy can maintain a sense of national cohesion and unity unless one school system is used to transmit a common culture to the next generation. A fifth is over whether religious groups have a right to use tax dollars to transmit their cultural capital to their children.

The victory of the Labor Party in Australian elections in December 1972 was due in part to its policy regarding school funding. A series of compromises subsequently resulted in providing governmental financial aid to both public and private schools. The Australian equivalent of the United States Supreme Court has upheld governmental aid to private schools.[7]

What will be the context for this public-policy debate in the United States in the early years of the twenty-first century? Will the "school question" be framed in terms of identifying a common enemy? Or in terms of the rights of parents and religious groups in an increasingly pluralistic democracy?

Or should the public-policy debate be on whether or not today's large public high schools should be classified as successes or as failures?

That is an exceptionally subjective question and merits a new chapter.

153

Chapter Ten

WHAT DO THEY DO BEST?

Given the absence of widespread agreement on a single core reason for the existence of large public high schools, the power of tradition, and the lack of any broad-based criteria for evaluation, it is difficult to define what they do best.

From this observer's perspective, the one role for which most schools earn a grade of A+ is easy to identify. Given their limited resources for this role and the fact that it never was perceived as one of the core purposes, most schools have performed remarkably well as a combination therapy center and free medical clinic for students.

> **Most schools have performed remarkably well as a combination therapy center and free medical clinic for students.**

The massacre at Columbine High School in Littleton, Colorado, in April 1999 raised the public expectations for this role to completely unrealistic levels. The expectation that high schools should be able to identify and report the existence of emotionally disturbed youth is far, far outside what the adults working there are equipped to do. The overwhelming majority of paid staff were not trained for that responsibility! Relatively few have an earned doctorate in psychiatry or even in psychology. That type of screening was never a core reason for the creation of public high schools.

154

What Do They Do Best?

Nevertheless, most of the public schools in the United States have responded admirably to the challenge. They have identified vision and hearing problems. They have recognized the symptoms of dyslexia, attention deficit disorder, obesity, poor physical condition, hypoglycemia, and various emotional problems. Equally important, tens of thousands of teachers have accepted the role of confidant, counselor, friend, surrogate parent, and mature adult role model for youth in desperate need of such an adult-teenager relationship.

Second, a grade of at least A should be awarded to those schools that have been able to provide a structured role for teenagers who come from a disruptive and unstructured home life. A large body of research suggests that the search for structure in life is the most urgent issue for youth.[1] While this was never among the top five reasons for the financial subsidy for the public schools, if performance is measured against reasonable expectations, a grade of A is merited. The marching band, football, the debate team, the daily schedule, drama groups, and pep rallies are among the ways high schools do provide a sense of structure to life for youth coming from dysfunctional homes.

While it was never formally articulated as a core purpose, for more than a century the public high schools have been reasonably safe warehouses for storing youngsters in the 14-18 age bracket. For the most part, the public high school kept them out of trouble, out of the labor force, and out of college for four years.

From 1870–1940 the combination of a changing labor force, a limited demand by colleges and universities for students age 15, 16, and 17, child labor laws, and urbanization created a need for safe warehouses. The public high schools of that era deserve at least a grade of B+ for filling that vacuum.

One excuse for writing this book is that the public demand in the United States today is not for better warehouses for youth in their mid-teens, but for safer prisons, better athletic fields, and more effective learning environments.

Fourth, the public high schools' most obvious measurable success story in the twentieth century was, like the Post Office, to provide indoor and reasonably good paying jobs for adults. Between 1970 and 1998 the number of students enrolled in this nation's public high schools dropped by 3 percent, but the number of classroom teachers increased by 18% and the number of paid positions in the public high schools increased by nearly 20 percent. Those increases rate a grade of at least a B+.

A fifth success story of the second half of the twentieth century in subsidized public education in America represents a complete political reversal of earlier years. President Harry S. Truman was a vigorous proponent of federal financial aid to the public schools. A coalition of liberal Protestant denominational leaders plus the anti-Catholic sentiments of many conservatives defeated Truman's proposal. The second half of the twentieth century brought $120 billion in Title I financial aid beginning in 1965 plus the establishment of the Cabinet level Department of Education which was awarded a budget of $35 billion for the 2000 fiscal year.

As recently as 1950 that would have been perceived as an impossible dream. Such a radical change in American public policy in only fifty years probably deserves an A.

What Hasn't Worked?

From the earliest days of the tax-supported public high school in America many of the professional educators have contended that their number-one purpose was to prepare teenagers to be productive students in colleges or university. For decades this became something of a joke because fewer than one-third of all ninth graders ever earned a high school diploma. By 1965, however, one-half of the American population, age 25 and over, had completed four years of high school and nearly 10 percent had completed at least four years of college. By the mid-1990s slightly over 60 percent of all recent high schools graduates were enrolled, at least on a part-time basis, in an institution of higher education.

"Academic Standards Eased As a Fear of Failure Spreads." That headline on the front pages of the newspapers of 1999 provided one explanation for the increase in the graduation rates. That headline also explains why an increasing number of American citizens have concluded that the large public high school has not succeeded in preparing teenagers for college level work.

A generous estimate is that one-half of that 60 percent who go on to school are prepared for college level academic study when they enroll. The growing demand for remedial courses, for tutoring, and for "dumbing down" the curriculum suggests that the public high schools have been far from successful in fulfilling that mission.

One response to the failure of the public high schools to prepare students for college level work has been the decision by a growing number of colleges and universities to sponsor charter schools. The competition for academically qualified students is so intense that one solution is to create charter school "farm clubs." By the fall of 1999 more than 200 charter schools had been sponsored by universities to begin to fill this vacuum.[2]

Clifford Adelman in the United States Department of Education reports that the most dependable predictor on how high school graduates will do in college is the level of difficulty in the high school courses taken by a student. The more difficult those high school courses, the greater the probability that the student will be able to succeed in college and go on to graduate school. That predictor is a better indicator of future success in college or the university than race, nationality, family income, or level of parental education.

That means if the public high schools do not challenge students with difficult courses, one alternative is for universities to sponsor charter schools that will.

A second core purpose of the public high school was and is to prepare students to become productive members of the American labor force. The response of employers, the proliferation of employer-sponsored training programs for entry level jobs, and the increase of tax-supported vocational schools suggests that this has not been a great success story.

A third widely supported goal for the public high school was to equip teenagers to become active citizens in a democratic society. In November 1999 the National Assessment of Educational Progress, administered by the United States Department of Education, reported that 26 percent of high school seniors had a "proficient" level of knowledge of American government, 39 percent scored at a "basic" level, and 35 percent were below "minimum requirements." If 26 percent of the students reaching a "proficient" level in citizenship is considered a passing grade, the schools could be given a grade of C. If, however, 70 percent is required for a passing grade, the public high schools have failed that test.

The Twenty-sixth Amendment to the United States Constitution was ratified on July 1, 1971. This granted eighteen-year-olds the right to vote. The participation rate of eighteen- and nineteen-year-olds at the polls does not suggest that the public high schools have been overwhelmingly successful in transmitting the rights and responsibilities that accompany citizenship in a democratic society.

Nutritionists, advocates of a healthy lifestyle, and those concerned with risk reduction in health flunk the typical public high school cafeteria. They contend that experiential learning, which is a powerful pedagogical tool, is being used to teach high school students how to poison themselves. The increase in the proportion of teenagers who are classified as "obese" is at a record level and some call it a new epidemic. Whether that increase in obesity will reduce the life expectancy of babies born in the 1980–2005 era, and thus produce a favorable impact on the Social Security fund, is yet to be determined.

In several public high schools the net revenues from the coin-operated vending machine are designated for health education, but the products dispensed by those vending machines send a different message to students.

Finally, while not officially stated in these terms, one of the hopes was that the public high school not only would deal with the "raging hormone" issue, but also would prepare students for a healthy, happy, and enduring marriage.

While a cause-and-effect relationship cannot be established, two sets of statistics and one symbol suggest this also has been less than a great success story. First, the tripling in the divorce rate since 1960 has coincided with the increase in the proportion of Americans who have completed four years of high school. Second, that rise in the graduation rate has coincided with the increase in the proportion of teenagers who are sexually active. Third, the symbol of a new era is the tax-supported day care center in the large public high school created for the children of students.

While highly subjective and far from comprehensive, these ten criteria for evaluation raise two questions. First, as a matter of public policy, should the large public high school be declared a success or a failure?

Second, and closer to the central theme of this book, are those ten criteria the best ones to use in evaluating the large public high school and/or in designing a new system for a new millennium?

That question should be examined within the context of six radical proposals for change as well as in the final chapter on effective learning communities.

Chapter Eleven

SIX PRESSURES FOR RADICAL CHANGE

W hat will you be doing five years from now?" I asked a high school senior one January afternoon.

"Five years from now I expect to be in my first year of my graduate work for a doctorate in biomedical engineering," she quickly replied. "This fall I will be a freshman in engineering school."

"That sounds like a challenging career plan," I commented. "Week after week, where in your life today are you challenged to do what you have never done before and know you can't do?"

"Dance," she replied without hesitation.

"Dance?" I questioned. "Tell me more."

"I take dance lessons for three hours after school every Monday and Thursday. That is when I am really challenged to excel," she explained.

"Great!" I affirmed. "What is number two on your list of when and where you are challenged to excel?"

After a long reflective pause she replied, "I guess number two would be the public dance performances we offer every month, but they really are not as demanding as our practice sessions."

"How about in your high school?" I asked. "Where in school are you challenged to do your very best?"

"I go to West High," she answered. "There the emphasis is on graduation, not on excellence."

* * * * *

On another day in another state I asked a junior where he is challenged to do his very best.

160

"Football," was the instant reply. "I'm a tackle on the varsity team, and this past fall we made it to the quarter finals for the state championship in our division. We don't have as much talent as some of the other schools, but we have a coach who demands the best out of everyone, and that's what has made us a winning team."

"Who else in your high school projects high expectations of you?" I inquired.

"My career counselor," he replied. "She wants me to go to the University of Texas in Austin, but I don't think I will. My current plans call for me to go to Texas A&M."

"Why not UT in Austin?" I asked.

"I'm not sure I'm academically prepared for the competition at UT," he explained. "This school lets you get by pretty easily, except for football. I would rather graduate in four years from A&M than flunk out at Austin."

A Call for Higher Expectations

Perhaps 10 to 15 percent of the high school students I meet complain about the absence of high academic expectations in their public high school. Most joke about how easy it is, while others complain that the low standards will handicap them when they go on to college.

> **Perhaps 10 to 15 percent of the high school students I meet complain about the absence of high academic expectations in their public high school.**

One response is special classes for the gifted. Another is advanced-placement classes. A growing number of high schools now offer courses for college credit.

The central limitation in this response is in the ecological environment. Any attempt to create a high-performance unit within the culture of a low-expectation institution means pumping water up a very high and steep hill.

The Evolution of the American Public High School

Generation after generation has learned and relearned a simple lesson. If the goal is excellence, self-sacrifice, and instilling a sense of vocation, then the learning experiences must be conducted in the context of an isolated institution organized around high performance. In historical terms, the number-one example has been officer training academies for military organizations. That list also includes medical schools, the top-quality law schools, the most effective theological seminaries (as contrasted with university-related divinity schools), and, most recently, state-wide and tax-funded residential high schools for those gifted in science and mathematics.

While it will be vulnerable to charges of being elitist and antiegalitarian, the most effective response to meeting this demand by teenagers for a high-expectation high school is to create geographically separate institutions with a low threshold for dismissal and high academic expectations. These could be the preparatory schools for students planning to enroll in an academically demanding college or university.

These would not be the same as the "magnet schools" that offer a specialized course of study for teenagers. The differences include (1) the distinction between a general education and a specialized education and (2) the level of expectations projected of the students.

The creation and operation of these academically demanding high schools include these three assumptions: (1) The majority, and perhaps the vast majority, of the teenagers in that school district will decide, "That is not the school for me. I'm not that committed to being a student." (2) The threshold for admission will be high with a low exit threshold. (3) Very high standards will be used in the selection and retention of faculty.

Redefining the Client

A second radical proposal for change came from a small number of professional educators in 1999 in their Statement of Principles for School Reform.

In addition to calling for an end to the public school monopoly and an affirmation of teaching as a profession, not as a job, the statement declares, "Children are the reason for education and [the] system's need must never take precedence over the needs of children."

> **The system's need must never take precedence over the needs of children.**

Challenging the Curriculum

The best organized, and perhaps the most powerful, of these six pressures for radical change is the recent surge in interest in learning by doing, rather than via lectures and the memorization of facts. One of the fundamental assumptions of this movement is that the pedagogical methods used in college with nineteen-year-olds may not be effective with fifteen-year-olds. (Whether they are effective with nineteen-year-olds is a subject for someone else's book.)

A second assumption is that the traditional curriculum-driven approach has been counterproductive.[1] The replacement for that approach is an inquiry-based methodology that emphasizes experiential and discovery learning plus teamwork.

Thus far, with six big historical exceptions, the focus on this new approach has been on the teaching of mathematics and science. That does not mean, however, that this approach cannot be implemented in every area of learning.

The six big exceptions, of course, where this hands-on approach to experiential learning has been utilized in public high schools for generations are basketball, shop, home economics, baseball, the immersion approach to learning a second language, and football. (See chapter 12 for more on the football model.)

A Change in Control

Perhaps the most significant statement that will accelerate the pace of ending the monopoly of the public schools on tax funds for education came from Sandra Feldman, president of the American Federation of Teachers. In her monthly column, "Where We Stand," in August 1999, Feldman suggested that the contracts between teachers' unions and school districts include one additional provision. This would grant to the teachers and administrators of each school the authority and responsibility to "meet statewide standards for learning and guarantee that schools have the resources they need to meet these goals."[2] The teachers and principals of each school would have the authority to hire the staff required to implement the customized strategy developed for their school.

This is a radical proposal for reform! It includes at least a half dozen highly commendable ideas. The first is the need to customize a strategy for each school rather than follow the "one size fits all" illusion. Second, it would be a badly needed vote of confidence in the competence, creativity, and dedication of the classroom teachers.[3] Third, it would enable the transfer of large sums of money now used to staff and operate the central district headquarters to be used in enriching the classroom learning environment. Fourth, it would be consistent with the current American societal trend to place greater authority and responsibility in the people who are doing the work the organization was created to do. (These last two features may doom its possible adoption. People in positions of authority and those who control the allocation of financial resources usually are reluctant to surrender these powers.)

Fifth, this proposal would facilitate a potentially crucial change in the questions used in evaluation. The current system of evaluation tends to focus on "How is your public school system doing?" This naturally leads to an emphasis on such specific input issues as the tax base, financial support, enrollment trends, the effectiveness of public relations efforts, the relationships between the superintendent and the board of education, the proportion of teachers with a post-graduate degree, salary schedules, the length of the school day, the quality and adequacy of the real estate, litigation, the length of the school year, the systems for transporting students, including bus schedules and student parking, the record of the high school varsity football and basketball teams, the number of academic courses taught by teachers who do not have the required academic preparation for teaching that course, and, whether the teachers are happy.

Feldman's proposal could change the focus of the evaluation process to one central question that focuses on outcomes: How are the students doing? Instead of attempting to hold a complicated and impersonal bureaucratic structure accountable for the students' performance, the principal and teachers of each school would be accountable. (A pilot project was launched in Denver in 1999 to tie teachers' compensation to students' performance rather than to tenure or academic credentials.)

Finally, as it now stands, Feldman's proposal probably is politically unacceptable. (In addition to threatening the status quo and the jobs of thousands of people in the central offices of every large public school system, it is vulnerable on the issue of accountability.)

The American political system traditionally has required those who provide public-funded services to be accountable to an elected body such as a city council or a board of education or the state legislature or the Congress or a regulatory body or a single elected official, such as a mayor or a governor, or, at a minimum, to the constituency served by that publicly funded agency. It appears that Feldman's proposal does not include that type of accountability. That could be a major asset!

In order to win the political support required to implement it, a tradeoff probably will be necessary. That trade-off could be to open the door to accountability in the educational marketplace. That would be consistent with a democratic society and a capitalistic economy. It also could earn broad-based political support for the heart of Feldman's proposal to expand the degree of control granted to teachers.

In more specific terms, the trade-off for the adoption of this proposal could be to terminate the monopoly the public school systems have had in the allocation of tax dollars for education. That local board of education could determine the annual financial subsidy for each student on a grade-by-grade basis and for

165

those in special education programs. The consumers of those educational services would determine the total annual public subsidy to every school, either public or private, by where they chose to enroll. That would mean that under Feldman's proposal the teachers and staff of every public school would have the freedom to design and implement a customized strategy for that school. Instead of being accountable to a state board of education or to the officials of that school district, however, they would be accountable to the parents and students who chose that school. The educational marketplace would replace the educational bureaucracy as the central point of accountability. This parallels what already is underway in the delivery of health-care services, in the competition for recruits for military service, in commercial air travel, in the transportation and delivery of packages, in higher education, and in all-day child care.

Feldman's proposal also could have strong appeal to those who place "saving the free, tax-supported public school" at the top of the list of priorities.

Rapid and successful implementation of her proposal could perpetuate the institutional life of perhaps 70 percent of all public schools in the United States. Stonewalling all efforts calling for innovation and reform may result in the eventual disappearance of all but 20 to 30 percent of today's public schools.

The choice for the United States Postal Service, for movie houses, for commercial airlines, for automobile manufacturers, for religious congregations, for grocery stores, for farmers, for long-distance trucking companies, for four-year private liberal arts colleges, for deliverers of health-care services, and for public schools is to adapt or die.

Sandra Feldman's proposal suggests to this observer that another alternative may be to adapt, to focus on a smaller market share, and to live happily ever after.

The Demand for Choices

The fifth of these six pressures for radical change is a product of a consumer-driven society. As recently as the 1950s choice was widely perceived as a luxury. Today choice is viewed as an entitlement.

In one generation cable television has expanded the range of choices available to consumers twentyfold. Restaurants, new car dealers, recruiters for the military services, discount stores, pharmacies, video rental stores, movie houses, cereal makers, motels, megachurches, supermarkets, major league professional sports leagues, and public libraries are among the many institutions that have taught younger generations that they have a right to more choices. The best single hope for perpetuating the tax-subsidized and traditional large general public high school of 1980 is that most of the fourteen-year-olds of 2010 will be the children of parents born before 1980, who were taught, "The world offers you two choices: Take it or leave it," and who will be able to transmit that worldview to the fourteen-year-olds of 2010.

A more likely scenario is that most of those fourteen-year-olds of 2010 will be the children of parents born after 1955, who were reared in a culture filled with competing choices. A reasonable prediction is that the fourteen-year-olds of 2010 will have far more choices than were available to the fourteen-year-olds of 1990 or 2000. The big unknown is what proportion of those students in the mid-teens will be enrolled in tax-supported "general education" public high schools with an enrollment of 500 or more. In 1998 those schools accounted for approximately three-quarters of the students in all high schools, both public and private, in the United States. In 2010 will that proportion be 85 percent? Or 75 percent? Or 60 percent? Or 40 percent? Or 20 percent?

The other half of that question is: Where will the others be enrolled? In accredited, diploma-granting virtual high schools organized around distance learning, such as the University of Missouri at Columbia High School or the Indiana University High School or the University of Nebraska at Lincoln High School? In distance learning centers operated by a public high school? In tax-funded high schools on Native American reservations? In an all-girl, tax-supported science and mathematics academy? In church-sponsored parochial schools funded out of a parish budget? In Christian day schools funded largely by parent- (and grandparent-) paid tuition? In Christian high schools funded by tax dollars? In parent- and teacher-sponsored charter schools financed largely by tax dollars? In corporation-sponsored charter schools financed largely by tax dollars? In corporation-sponsored charter schools, such as the Ryder Charter School in Dade County, Florida? In charter schools sponsored by civic groups, including parents? In privately sponsored military schools? In publicly financed military high schools, such as those opened recently by the Chicago public school system? In private four-year college preparatory schools? In publicly financed college preparatory schools operated by public school districts? In college preparatory schools operated by colleges and universities? In both public and private Waldorf schools? In very large "general" public high schools of the 1998 model in which 30 to 60 percent of the seniors fail the state-mandated test required for earning a diploma? In four-year high schools with an enrollment under 500 in which every student spends four years studying Latin plus at least three years studying Greek plus at least three years studying French or German? In four-year high schools with all-day child care for the children of students? In small high schools that place a high priority on encouraging every student to be an active member of a group, team, or board that shares in a common task and that is marked by a strong emphasis on high expectations, discipline, rules, boundaries, creativity, team work, and helping others? In vocational schools operated by public school districts? In private vocational schools operated by for-profit organizations? In distance learning centers operated by churches and other nonprofit organizations? In distance learning centers operating by a public school system? In seven-day-a-week residential settings operated by a charitable organization, such as the Hershey school in Pennsylvania?[4] In five- or six- or seven-day-a-week residential (boarding) high schools for youth from severely dysfunctional home environments that are operated by a public school district or by the state? In a high school operated by the state for gifted youth who want to specialize in mathematics and science? In a high school designed for emotionally disturbed (or severely physically handicapped or prone to violent antisocial behavior) teenagers operated by a private corporation, but publicly funded? In a publicly funded high school for youth who want to specialize in music and drama? In a publicly funded high school for youth who want to be equipped for a job on the information highway? In a high school organized around the teaching theme of "directed learning"? In a home schooling environment enriched by distance learning and partially subsidized by tax dollars? In smalltown and rural, tax-supported public high schools with an enrollment under 300? In urban and suburban public high schools designed for fewer than 500 students? In "immersion language" public high schools designed to produce fluent bilingual and trilingual graduates? In tax-supported high schools operated by a university school of education? In a mid-sized public high school designed for teenagers who want to become professional athletes? In a privately financed Jewish high school?[5] In a four-year public high school with an enrollment of 300 to 500 that is one of several separate and self-governing small high schools housed in a building originally designed for a four-year high school with 2,000 to 5,000 students, but remodeled to accommodate several separate schools? In a small to midsized public school for youth who have never experienced success that is designed to enable every student to be able to declare, "I can do that better than nine out of ten of my peers"? In a small high school designed to help youth with IQs of 90-110 earn a good grade on college-entrance examinations and operated by a for-profit corporation? In a high school designed for recent immigrants, ages 14-17, to help them master the English language while acquiring an education? In a high school that specializes in preparing students to work in the construction industry or as mechanics or a similar vocation? In a school designed for terminal formal education at grade 9 or 10 as in Germany?

That is a long paragraph that probably overlooks at least a dozen options that will be open to the fourteen-year-olds of 2010. The two big differences between 1990 and 2010 is that in

2010 that list of different types of high schools will be twice as long as it was in 1990, and there will be a larger number of high schools in each category.

Change the Culture

The history of the public high school in twentieth-century America can be divided into three chapters. One recounts the rapid growth in enrollment. A second describes the still unresolved quarrel over the definition of purpose and the appropriate pedagogical culture. A third chapter could recapture the endless efforts at reform.

These three chapters could lead the critic to conclude that maybe this was a bad idea from the very beginning and that the time has come to close out that dysfunctional institution. A more creative response could be to look around and ask, Has any other large institution that had as its primary constituency young Americans ever been able to reform itself?

One answer is yes: the United States Marine Corps. During the Vietnam war the Marine Corps endured more casualties than it had in World War II, experienced serious internal conflict, and suffered from an erosion of morale. The 1970s saw the Corps undermined by racial violence. Drug abuse was a widespread problem. At one point fewer than one-half of all recruits were high school graduates.

During the past two decades, however, the Marine Corps has been transformed. How was that accomplished? One answer is the Corps was reformed—and transformed—by a renewed emphasis on its distinctive culture, which is organized around a clearly defined value system. Honor, discipline, courage, commitment, high expectations, sacrifice, order, teamwork, and "always faithful" are at the heart of that value system.[6]

In many large public high schools a similar value system is a central organizing principle in the marching band, the varsity football team, and sometimes in the varsity basketball team, the varsity soccer team, and the science or math team that enters a national contest.

Six Pressures for Radical Change

One alternative is to reform every public school system around values. Replace the bureaucratic structure as the central organizing principle with a clearly defined value system and a culture of learning.

Three Alternatives

An incremental alternative is to create new public high schools in the existing public school system that are organized around structure, a distinctive institutional culture, high expectations, learning, discipline, honor, courage, creativity, self-reliance, sacrifice, order, teamwork, and commitment.

That would be a far easier strategy to implement than to attempt to transform the culture and instill a new value system in an existing public high school. It is always easier to create the new than to reform the old!

It is always easier to create the new than to reform the old!

A second alternative would be to allocate tax dollars to fund the creation of new values-driven charter schools.

The fastest strategy to implement would be to subsidize both public and private values-driven, high-expectation-driven high schools.

How long should the babies born back in 1987 and 1988 be asked to wait before they will have the option of enrolling in a tax-funded high school that (1) projects high academic expectations of everyone who chooses that school; (2) is organized on the assumption that the student, not the system, is the number-one client; (3) is designed for hands-on experiential learning; (4) affirms, supports, and rewards the classroom teachers as the most valuable employees; (5) is organized to affirm, support, and perpetuate a values-driven culture; and (6) rewards both individual performance and teamwork?

The Evolution of the American Public High School

Another way to state the issue is to ask, What is an effective learning community?

That requires a visit to a mythical high school that includes on the staff several composite personalities taken from real life.

This visit also will demonstrate that effective learning communities do exist within schools that are not high-performance organizations—but that requires writing a new rule book for a new and different game. Writing that new rule book for a new game is an essential component of any strategy for incremental change initiated from within any large and tradition-driven institution. Carl Swanson and Helen Highwater are models of how to write and follow a new rule book in an old and obsolete ecological environment.

For those who prefer a real-life model of writing a new rule book on how to be an effective and happy teacher with today's teenagers, the most highly visible example is the National Teacher of the year for 2000. Ms. Marilyn Whirrey, who teaches American literature in a high school in California, is an inspiring model of a teacher who combines a love for teenagers with a passion for teaching, a recognition of the power of small groups, a profound understanding of the impact of the ecological environment, a conviction that learning can be a contagious and joyous experience, a Socratic pedagogical style, and a creative mind. Ms. Whirrey also has discovered that a desk is not an essential piece of furniture in a classroom and that large beanbags can be a comfortable substitution for chairs. Ms. Whirrey is one of thousands of teachers who are the real-life versions of Helen Highwater.

Chapter Twelve

WHAT IS A LEARNING COMMUNITY?

I t is a beautiful Tuesday in early September at Washington High School. This public high school has an enrollment of 1155 students scattered over four grades. A sophomore class in American Literature is offered twice a day by 25-year-old Terry Adams in Room 227. Terry also teaches three first-year composition courses. The early morning American Literature class has an enrollment of 29 and the late morning class includes 28 students.

The students in the class that begins at 7:40 every morning have concluded they have five choices. Nearly one-third are able and willing to make the effort to learn how to learn from the pedagogical style chosen by the teacher. That opens the door for them to learn what Terry Adams knows about American literature. They may not master the subject, but they can learn all Terry Adams knows about that slice of American literature. It is clear to Terry and to everyone else in the room these are eager learners.

Two or three students at that early hour choose an adversarial stance and openly challenge nearly everything the teacher says or does. One explains, "That's the only way I can stay awake. I didn't get to bed until nearly midnight last night, and I have to catch the school bus at 7:05 every morning." Another explains, "I hate this course, and I was taught to fight what you hate."

Several other students are practicing the skill of sleeping with their eyes open. They are bored, sleepy, and eager to get this chore behind them. A couple of others engage in various forms of disruptive behavior. They enjoy testing the limits. How far can we go without being sent to the principal's office by this young teacher?

The remaining four or five appear to be taking notes. In fact, one is working on the ideal box score for his favorite baseball team. A second is writing a letter. A third is outlining a novel she plans to write. A fourth is calculating how to spend Friday's paycheck from his weekend job in a fast food restaurant.

That first hour class includes an unusually large proportion of highly self-motivated, intellectually gifted, and articulate fifteen-year-olds. Terry Adams often refers to this as "my best class." At times the competition is described by several students as "cutthroat, but I enjoy it. Despite the early hour, that class gets my day off to a great start!"

A different reaction is expressed by four or five boys. "That class has too many preppies and eager beavers in it! They come to school to make the rest of us feel really stupid. Getting up early to catch the school bus and then going into that room with those nerds who want to show off how much they know really gets my day off to a lousy start!"

That is but one example of how the same ecological environment can evoke two radically different evaluations.

When the principal at Washington High School was asked about Terry Adams, he immediately held up three fingers and replied, "First of all, Terry has a passion for American literature. I wish all our classroom teachers displayed that same level of passion for their subject. Second, Terry really is a scholar. Like many other scholars, Terry is on the introverted side of the personality scale. Third, Terry really is misplaced here. Terry really should be teaching graduate students in a research university. Doctoral students need a scholarly mentor. Our teenagers here need a loving friend."

In another room in that same building on that Tuesday afternoon, forty-seven-year-old Carl Swanson, the football coach, explains to a group of teenagers, "Well, we lost

174

our first game of the season last Friday night. They have a good team, but I was hoping we could beat them. As I've explained to all of you before, you have two choices here. The first, which is what we teach, is about learning how to play winning football. We're not teaching a physical fitness class. We're committed to teaching you how to learn to be a contributing member of a winning football team. We all need to learn how to lose and to survive defeat, but that's not our primary goal in this program. Our goal is for you to learn how to be a contributing member of a winning team. That word *team* is of equal importance to that word *winning*. Football is a team sport!

"This is my seventh year as the head football coach here at Washington, and as you all know, everyone who comes out for football makes the squad. We don't cut anyone. As long as you want to learn, you'll be on the squad. You may not play in every game, but you'll play in every practice. You cut yourself when you decide you don't want to learn. Am I clear? Any questions?"

Three of the boys in that 7:40 A.M. American Literature class are also on that football squad. Everyday, for five days a week, these three boys are experiencing two vastly different learning environments.

What Are the Differences?

1. The most obvious difference is the time of day. That American Literature class is scheduled at an early hour for the convenience of the school bus system. For many of those teenagers, their biological clocks call for them to awaken about a half hour after the conclusion of that class. The football coach takes them out on the practice field at the ideal time of the day for strenuous physical activity.

2. All of the students in that American Literature class are required to have four years of English to graduate. Nearly all of the candidates for the football team are self-motivated volunteers who want to play football. (Two or three may be there to

please their father or to emulate an older brother, but they are the exceptions.)

3. One of the most subtle, and extremely significant differences is what these teenagers are expected to learn. Early that morning those students are expected to learn (a) how to learn from the pedagogical style followed by Terry Adams, (b) American literature, and (c) how to function as an individual learner.

Coach Swanson has designed a system that emphasizes (a) how to learn how to be a contributing member to a team effort, (b) how to master the skills of playing a particular position, (c) how to learn from peers, and (d) how to learn from one's mistakes.

Terry Adams designs one lesson plan to fit 28 or 29 students. Coach Swanson must design several different lesson plans—one for quarterbacks, one for wide receivers, one for linebackers, etc.

4. That distinction between learning as an individual and learning as a team is reinforced by the physical environment. Terry Adams meets in a room in which each student sits in an individual chair with a wide arm for writing. The room is designed on the assumption that one size fits all, one lesson plan fits everyone, and learning should be an individual effort.

Down on the first floor of Washington High is Helen Highwater's classroom, which she designed when this building was being planned. Forty-five-year-old Mrs. Highwater is in her twenty-third year teaching history in this district. She teaches three sections of American history and two classes of world history. She insisted her room be designed to accommodate eight tables with up to five students at each one. Her pedagogical style calls for the students to work in teams of three or five. Each team "owns" its own table for that period. All assignments, except for reading at home and three tests per semester, are undertaken and completed by teams. Everyone at the same table receives the same grade on a particular assignment. Peer pressure becomes a powerful motivating force for learning. "My grade depends on how well the rest of you dummies at my table do."

What Is a Learning Community?

Mrs. Highwater uses a baseball analogy to explain the difference between a focus on individual performance and teamwork. It is the seventh inning, the score is tied, and bases are loaded with one out. The count on the batter is three balls and two strikes. The pitcher, who is an individualist, believes the ideal pitch is one that will produce a called third strike. The manager wants a pitch that will result in a ground ball to the shortstop for an easy double play. Do we depend largely on ourselves or do we depend heavily on our teammates?

Until recently baseball records tended to exalt individual performances such as batting averages, home runs, strikeouts, runs batted in, and earned-run averages. Should the reward system in high school lift up individual performance? Or teamwork? Or both?

Should the reward system in high school lift up individual performance? Or teamwork? Or both?

Nine members of this year's football squad are taking a history course with Mrs. Highwater. Coach Swanson identifies her as one of his few allies in helping boys learn how to be contributing members of a winning team.

When Coach Swanson takes those teenagers out on the practice field, he has an ideal ecological environment for (a) helping students to learn and practice teamwork, (b) challenging everyone to master individual skills, (c) grabbing and holding the attention of every player, and, (d) perhaps most important of all, implementing individualized lesson plans designed to build on the gifts, skills, physical characteristics, personality, and dreams of each candidate for that team.

To succeed, Coach Swanson must identify and build on the assets each student brings to that learning environment.

Terry Adams is expected to teach a subject called American Literature.

5. "Success" for Terry Adams's class means every student

earns a passing grade in American Literature. "Success" for Carl Swanson requires challenging every member of the squad to fulfill his or her individual potential and helping that youngster achieve that goal, plus blending all those gifts, personalities, and skills into the creation of a cohesive team.

6. Most of those football players want to learn how to play football. A few of Terry Adams' students want to learn more about the contribution of the great American writers, but most are there because an authority figure, whom they have never met, has decided they must be exposed to four years of high school English to graduate.

7. The candidates for the Washington High football team watch college and professional football games on television. Those experiences reinforce and affirm what Coach Swanson teaches. Those televised games also enable the students to (a) see that they are in an adult world of endeavor, (b) see what perfection looks like, and (c) learn from the mistakes of others.

Occasionally Terry Adams will recommend a particular television program the students should watch that will expand their knowledge of American literature, but only rarely will even one-half of the students fulfill that assignment. No one, including Terry Adams and the fathers of the students in that class, ever watches eight to ten hours of television programs on American literature in any one weekend. At least a few teenagers determine what is important by looking at their father's priorities in life.

8. A winning season for the Washington High football team produces important satisfactions for all the players, including those who averaged only two minutes of playing time per game. Many of the parents also derive feelings of satisfaction from that success.

It is rare to see a local newspaper headline declaring, "Washington High American Literature Class Completes Season Undefeated." In fact, there is some dispute over the definition of a winning season for a high school American Literature class.

9. After a few games, and perhaps even earlier, Coach

Swanson's football squad consists of the starters, the second string, and the "wanabees." Those who came out for football but refused to attempt to meet the high expectations projected by the coach are gone.

As the semester nears an end, Terry Adams' class includes winners, active malcontents, bored and passive attenders, plus at least a few self-identified losers.

10. The football players at Washington High are expected to act like young adults. That adult orientation is reinforced by the number of adult spectators at the Friday night games, by the televised university and professional games, and by the attitude of Coach Swanson and his assistants.

Several of the students in Terry Adams' class feel they are being treated as children.

11. Each of these three teachers does have help. Every semester Terry Adams has a senior from the school of education at the near-by university. This semester that student is a 21-year-old woman who always arrives before 7:25 A.M. but has to leave immediately after the second period to attend her classes at the university ten miles to the east. Near the end of the semester, under Terry's supervision, she will prepare the lesson plan and teach a week-long unit. Most of the time, however, she is really a flunky.

Helen Highwater's aide, Elizabeth Benton, who majored in American history in college but does not have any academic teaching credentials, became Helen's partner nine years ago. Elizabeth is a financially well-off, sixty-one-year-old widow with seven grandchildren. She works nearly full-time for part-time compensation. She and Helen have become close personal friends. Helen NEVER refers to Elizabeth as "my aide." The reference always is to "my partner." They work as a collegial team. Whenever Helen is absent, Elizabeth uses the lesson plans they have prepared together and performs at a superior level in teaching those classes. Helen sometimes describes Elizabeth as "my alter ego." This semester Helen Highwater's classes have a combined enrollment of 166 students, but several are enrolled in both her American history class and her world history class.

The Evolution of the American Public High School

When asked to describe Mrs. Highwater, the principal held up five fingers and replied, "First of all, Helen has a passion for helping adolescents mature into healthy and happy young adults. She and her husband had two children who graduated from here. They were two of the psychologically best-adjusted young people I have ever met.

"Second, Helen and Elizabeth Benton are the best model of a cooperative partnership we have here. They are both high energy and loving people. You walk into that classroom and you can feel the energy, enthusiasm, and love that fills the room. It's contagious and, at least for one period every day, the kids catch that enthusiasm. The discipline problems in Helen's class are as close to zero as you can get in today's world.

"Third, when this new building was being designed to replace the old high school built back in 1958, Helen demanded a voice in that process. She picked a classroom at the opposite end of the building from the cafeteria. She chose the furniture and the furnishings. She wanted an inside room with windows on only one side. She wanted lots of blank walls. She believes the walls teach. Last spring, when there were no students in the building because it was one of two days in the semester set aside for continuing education for our teachers, I asked my secretary to go in and inventory what was on those walls.

"In addition to several dozen maps, charts, and graphs, which Helen and Elizabeth change every few weeks, my secretary counted 187 pieces of various colored seven-by-nine inch sheets of paper. Most were posted between four and six feet above the floor. On each sheet was a quotation from an individual student or study team with the person's or team's name in smaller letters. Helen and Elizabeth had extracted these one- and two-sentence quotations from papers the students had written or research projects completed by a team or statements made orally. Each one lifted up a specific insight or bit of wisdom or observation. It took her more than half the day, but my secretary checked against the class enrollment sheets and discovered that every student's name was up on the wall at least once, either individually or as a member of a team. Well over a hundred had something with their name on it posted at least twice, but none more than twice. This was on the fifth week of the semester! That meant that when a student came into that classroom, they felt, "I belong here. My name is on the wall. I have made a contribution to the learning environment in this room." Talk about affirmation, inclusion, and belonging. Helen's room tells every student, You belong here!

"In addition, whenever a student transfers into Washington High during the school year and enrolls in one of Helen's clases, an 8" x 10" color photograph of that newcomer with a brief biographical sketch is posted on the wall within a few days.

"Of course, we can't give every teacher his or her own room," continued the principal, "but Helen is an exception who deserves exceptional treatment. Carl Swanson, for example, shares one of our science rooms with three other science teachers.

"A fourth characteristic of Mrs. Highwater is her passion for history. She makes what many kids see as a dull subject as exciting as a movie about tomorrow.

"Finally, as you already know, Helen has organized her classes, as much as the system permits, to be a collection of teams, rather than a collection of individual students. That is one reason why she has so few discipline problems. She has created an environment that channels peer pressures into positive channels. If we could clone Helen and Elizabeth to staff every teaching position in this high school, I wouldn't be needed. Fortunately for my family's economic well-being, that is not yet possible.

"You also should know that the reason Helen *qualifies* for an aide is because her classes average 32 to 35 in enrollment. The reason she *needs* an aide is because each class consists of seven or eight teams. Coaching seven different teams constitutes a bigger work load than teaching thirty-five students."

For many of the students, the gregarious Helen Highwater is their surrogate mother and that loving partner is their surrogate grandmother. This is especially important for five boys who are being reared by single-parent fathers, for eleven girls who are being reared by their biological fathers and by stepmothers, and for at least three dozen other students who come from unhappy home environments.

Coach Swanson, who teaches three biology classes every morning, has two paid assistants. The twenty-seven-year-old also teaches economics and the forty-nine-year-old also teaches physics. Coach Swanson is also an assistant to the basketball head coach in the winter and an assistant to the baseball head coach in the spring.

In addition to the two paid assistants, Coach Swanson depends on two volunteers. One is a sixty-five-year-old retired father of four daughters who coached college football for nine years. The other volunteer assistant coach is a retired former National Football offensive lineman. This sixty-one-year-old volunteer has a grandson who is a second string tackle on the Washington High football squad.

These five coaches provide these teenage boys with two surrogate grandfather figures, two surrogate father figures, and one surrogate big brother figure. This is especially important to the nine boys on the squad who are being reared by single-parent mothers and the two who are being reared by grandmothers.

12. One of the subtle, but extremely significant differences in these learning environments is Coach Swanson is operating within the context of a clearly defined moral contract. While stated more gently than this, that contract conveys the message, "Shape up or ship out." The five coaches understand that they have a moral obligation to help every boy fulfill his potential as a person, as a player, and as a member of the team. They want every player to learn to excel, but they also recognize that only those who want to learn can excel. The players all understand that fulfilling their potential requires hard work and an eagerness to learn.

Terry Adams operates within the context of a contract based on the clock. "You give me fifty minutes of your time, and I'll give you my best for those fifty minutes. What you learn is up to you."

Helen Highwater operates with a two-paragraph contract. "We love you and we want you to learn. You can show your love for us by learning how to learn.

"Mrs. Benton and I work together as a team, and we want you

182

to learn how to work with others as a team. Your success will be determined in large part by how effective you are as a contributing member of a team. That is true for this class, and that probably will apply, when the time comes, to your marriage and to how you earn a living."

13. While it is clearly an unfair advantage, Coach Swanson functions with a learning environment that is reinforced by the active and supportive cooperation of more than two dozen fathers.

14. While this overlaps a couple of the other distinctions, it cannot be emphasized too strongly that two-fifths of Terry Adams' job can be defined as teaching American literature while three-fifths is teaching English composition. Coach Swanson and his colleagues understand that an essential component of their learning environment requires them to focus on helping students learn how to learn.

15. One of the crucial differences is that from a pedagogical perspective the students in Mrs. Highwater's class and the players on the football squad are given the opportunity to experience two forms of success. One is individual learning. The other is to learn how to be a contributing member of a team.

By contrast, success in that American Literature class is based on individual learning. The "cutthroat competition" provided by one-third of the class enhances that emphasis on individual learning, but it also intimidates several students.

16. From a teacher's perspective the biggest difference among these scenarios is that Terry Adams was set up to fail. Three years ago the innocent Terry Adams accepted an exceptionally difficult assignment that included three components. The first was to teach required courses to students, most of whom were not eager volunteers to learn that subject. An old cliche declares, "It is impossible to teach an adult anything that adult does not want to learn." It also is difficult to teach a fifteen-year-old anything that teenager does not want to learn.

Second, Terry brought a pedagogical methodology designed for teaching American literature to twenty- and twenty-one-year-old university student volunteers to the assignment of teaching a required course to fifteen-year-olds.

183

Third, the combination of the ecological environment of that classroom, the social setting, and culture of Washington High, Terry's pedagogical methodology, and the content of the subject matter combined with the sentence mandated by state law that fourteen- and fifteen-year-olds must be enrolled in and attend school set Terry up to fail.

By contrast, Coach Swanson was given an ecological environment that made his assignment far easier. While he was not guaranteed success, he could swim with a strong tide. Terry Adams was assigned to swim against an even stronger tide.

Many years earlier a younger, enthusiastic, and energetic Helen Highwater was hired by Washington High to teach history. She also brought with her a university classroom model of how to teach history to twenty- and twenty-one-year-old history majors. Within a few months Helen concluded that the model was encountering serious resistance when used with teenagers, most of whom did not identify themselves as history majors. Gradually she created a new design that came closer to matching her gifts and personality with her assignment.

When that school district decided to replace that old and obsolete high school building with a new structure, Helen *demanded*, she did not simply ask for, the opportunity to design a room that would be a more compatible ecological environment with her approach to team learning, peer responsibility, student initiative, affirmation of learning, inclusion, and competition.

(Incidentally, when Helen was told her principal strongly affirmed her style of team teaching, she replied, "If I've told him once, I told him a hundred times that is *not* what Elizabeth and I are doing! Elizabeth and I model a team approach to our assignment, but our focus is on team learning, not on team teaching!"

> **When Helen was told her principal strongly affirmed her style of team teaching, she replied, "Our focus is on team learning, not on team teaching!"**

What Is a Learning Community?

In recent years Helen also has brought another valuable lesson to her classroom. She and her husband have happily survived the rearing of two teenagers. Those experiences have greatly enriched her competence in working with the contemporary generation of teenagers.

Like Terry, Helen walked into an ecological environment and a social setting, was given a constituency and subject matter, and brought with her a pedagogical methodology, which, when combined, were designed to produce boredom in most teenagers. Systems produce what systems are designed to produce! That system was designed to produce alienation, boredom, and disruptive behavior. Helen possessed the insight, the courage, and the determination to discard that dysfunctional system. She replaced it with a healthy and constructive system designed to produce cooperation, creativity, participation, competition, learning, enthusiasm, a sense of inclusion, a feeling of belonging, and a compatible reward plan.

Coach Swanson explains, "Helen has been pumping water up a steep hill here for twenty-five years. One reason she is such a great teacher is she never stops pumping."

A Second Look at Football

When asked about Coach Swanson, the fifty-eight-year-old principal at Washington High held up five fingers and enthusiastically declared, "First, Carl is driven by a passion to challenge and help every youngster who comes out for football to fulfill that kid's potential. A key part of Carl's passion is to elevate the level of that self-identified potential. That also means Carl can focus on the unique gifts and personality of each youngster rather than on a subject.

"Second, Carl has a huge advantage over the classroom teacher, thanks to the importance people around here place on football. By definition, a winning football team is a high performance organization. A central characteristic of a high performance organization is a high threshold for admission or retention and a low exit threshold. Every student is welcome to come out for varsity football. Last year, for example, for the first time in the history of Washington High, several girls decided to come out for football. Carl welcomed them! Two made the team and each one, including the field goal kicker, played in every game. The threshold for retention, however, rises sharply after the first few days of workouts. An absence of determination, enthusiasm, discipline, or commitment leads well over half of those who come out to cross that low exit threshold within a week or two.

"By contrast," continues the principal, "state law requires us to have a very low threshold for admission into our academic classes and a high exit threshold. It's easy to get in and hard to get kicked out of a class here. Boredom is not an exit strategy from an English class, but boredom leads to the exit door if you want to play varsity football here.

"A second component of a high performance organization is competence in individual achievement ranks no higher than third in the hierarchy of values. Teamwork and a commitment to the overall performance of the team rank ahead of individual performance. That's one of the problems facing major league professional sports teams today. Several teams have a highly paid self-centered star with superb talent who places his personal statistics above a winning record for that team. That is not the way to build a high performance organization! Our large public high schools all across the country are filled with classrooms that place a premium on individual performance. That also may include the criteria used to evaluate the faculty.

"This means Coach Swanson operates within the context of a high performance institutional organization. It is relatively easy to create a challenging learning environment within a low performance organizational context."

"How would you describe Washington High?" I asked.

"This is a low performance organizational environment," came the instant reply. "State law requires that. We are forbidden by state law, as well as barred by other factors, from making this high school a high performance organization, but we can talk about that later.

186

What Is a Learning Community?

"A third big advantage Carl Swanson enjoys is very few of his players come from homes where everyone is completely disengaged from high school football," added this principal. "Nearly every player has at least one parent, or perhaps an older sibling, who comes to every home game. Most of the players have a family support system that includes two or three or four or five or more members. These include parents, grandparents, siblings, and cousins. A lot of them even come out to watch football practice after school, and some travel to the games away from home.

"My offhand guess is fewer than 80 percent of our students in our English or world history classes here at Washington High come from homes where there is an equal level of family engagement in the study of English or history.

"A fourth reason why everyone sees Carl as a great teacher is he and most of his players benefit from the continuity of the relationship of coach and players. In this state freshmen are eligible to play on the varsity teams. This means that for many of our seniors, this is their fourth year with him as their coach. Several also play on either the basketball or baseball teams where he is an assistant coach, and many have been or are in one of the biology classes he teaches. That continuity of relationships over a long period of time is a tremendously influential factor in creating a positive learning environment.

"Fifth, Carl takes advantage of the fast feedback that is a part of high school football. Most of the students in our academic classes occasionally receive feedback on their performance from tests, term papers, and their participation in classroom discussions. Mrs. Highwater has designed her classes so every student receives feedback from their peers every day as well as from her and Elizabeth, but that is an exception.

"The kids in Coach Swanson's football squad receive constructive feedback several times in every practice session as well as after every game. Feedback is a crucial component of an effective learning community. That represents one more advantage Carl has over the classroom teachers here."

If this principal had been blessed with ten fingers on his right hand, he could have added five more facets to that description of Coach Swanson's learning community.

1. Competition can be a useful motivator to elevate the performance level of both the individual and of the team. At Washington High players compete for a starting assignment on the varsity football team. Fewer than a dozen compete to be on the starting team in Terry Adams' classes.

2. The overall team goal, win the next game, is communicated in precise, measureable, and easy-to-understand language. What is the team goal for next week's American Literature class?

3. Character is a high value in the high performance organization. Coach Swanson repeatedly makes it clear to everyone on the squad that good character, clean sportsmanship, and individual responsibility are high values in his program.

Terry Adams has a far more difficult assignment in lifting up the importance of good character in those American Literature classes.

4. While high school football does not quite fit into the contemporary definition of an "extreme sport," it is far closer than baseball or golf. In the extreme sports, participants bond around that common task, rather than primarily around relationships. An infantry battle is the number-one example of an extreme sport. Participants bond with one another against a common enemy and in support of one another. Titles, seniority, age, and ancestry become unimportant. A parallel to the extreme sport is that group of young computer experts who work together in ninety-hour weeks to create and perfect new software. Work becomes fun. The whole effort is driven by a passion for what they are doing. Creating the Apple computer was an extreme sport.

This same point can be illustrated by the difficulties Mrs. Highwater and Mrs. Benton experience in their emphasis on teams. The study of world history is much closer to golf than it is to an extreme sport, such as covering 200 miles in a seven-day trip through a jungle and across a desert by walking, climbing, paddling, and running while carrying all your food, water, and other supplies for that trip. The study of world history is unlike working all night to complete a videotape to be shown at nine o'clock in the morning or meeting a deadline to launch a space vehicle.

Among the tactics used by Mrs. Highwater and Mrs. Benton are these: (1) The students choose whether they want to be a member of a three-person or a five-person team. (2) With a few obvious limitations each student choses his or her team. (3) On the third day of the semester, they draw straws to determine the order for each team to choose a table for its "place" for that semester. (4) On the fourth day of the semester a sheet is handed out to each team listing two dozen narrowly defined "lessons" and the date each lesson will be taught. The teams are given a week to choose the topic or lesson that team will teach in a twenty-five minute period during the first half of the semester and a second lesson to be taught during the second half of the semester. If two or more teams choose the same topic and date, they are expected to decide by themselves how to resolve that conflict. (5) The preliminary lesson plan for each topic is due one week before the scheduled presentation. (6) Mrs. Highwater and Mrs. Benton are available to coach each team on preparing that first preliminary lesson plan, but not on researching the content. (7) Each team will design its own pedagogical format for teaching their topic. (Since coaching a five-person team requires more time and a higher level of skill than coaching a three-person team, Mrs. Benton works with the three-person teams and Mrs. Highwater coaches the five-person teams.)

Mrs. Highwater is convinced of the wisdom in the old adage, "The best way to learn a subject is to teach it." She believes that peer pressure and competition can be positive components of an effective learning environment. She also is convinced that a team can be more creative than an individual and that teenagers can and do learn from one another. Mrs. Benton makes a videotape of each of those twenty-five-minute presentations. Each team is given the opportunity for a private (outside of class) viewing of their videotape. This component is based on the assumption that people can learn from reviewing their performance—the same assumption Coach Swanson follows for videotaping every football game.

5. Perhaps most important of all, Coach Swanson, like Mrs. Highwater, displays a strong sense of vocation. Teaching teenagers and coaching high school sports is clearly his calling. By contrast, Terry Adams has a job teaching American literature while going to graduate school during the summer.

Shared Convictions

Coach Swanson and Mrs. Highwater share several pedagogical convictions.

They both believe that the ecological environment is an influential component of an effective learning community.

They both believe that passion for a subject is contagious and can be modeled, but it cannot be taught.

They both believe that if young people can experience the joy of learning and the satisfactions of succeeding, they are well along the road to becoming lifelong learners.

They both believe that teams are the best instructors for helping people learn how to become contributing members of a team.

They both believe that competition and peer pressures can be constructive forces in an effective learning environment.

They both believe that teenagers can and do learn from one another.

They both believe that teenagers are more likely to enjoy learning if they are treated like adults rather than like children.

They both believe in the power of high expectations.

They both believe in the value of practice before the "big game."

They both believe that adults can be valuable coaches and mentors.

They both believe that the effective mentor regularly communicates to each person being mentored, usually by actions and relationships, "At this moment you are the most important person in my life, and you have my undivided attention."[1]

What Is a Learning Community?

They both believe that videotapes of a group (or individual) performance can be a valuable learning opportunity and that students can be expected to remain after school or come in on Saturday to learn from those videotapes.

They both believe that a sense of "belonging" opens the door for more effective learning.

A sense of "belonging" opens the door for more effective learning.

They both believe in the potential contributions of mature adult role models.

They both accept the role of surrogate parent, friend, counselor, confidant, or wise adult and feel comfortable in that role.

They both wish for greater parental involvement and support.

They both believe that they are fulfilling their vocational calling—teaching is NOT a job!

Teaching is NOT a job!

They both believe that every youngster can and should be challenged to excel in at least one facet of life.

They both believe that the higher the level of expectations projected by leaders, the higher the performance level of the participants.

They both believe that good character can be affirmed, modeled, and transmitted.

They both believe in the power of experiential learning, of learning by doing.

They both believe that challenging people to do what they have never done before and know they cannot do is both (a) the best antidote to boredom and (b) the best way to transform "ordinary teenagers" into persons fulfilling their potential.

They both believe that they are preparing teenagers for life in an adult-dominated world, not simply transmitting a body of knowledge about a particular subject.

They both enjoy being with teenagers.

They both affirm the value of hard work.

Most important of all, both Mrs. Highwater and Coach Swanson, like thousands of other high school teachers, are happiest and enjoy their greatest sense of fulfillment when they are free to practice what they believe.

Twelve Questions

1. Which of the three learning environments described earlier in this chapter is most likely to produce boredom?

2. Which of the three is most likely to provide a supportive environment for teenagers who feel alienated from the rest of the world?

3. Which is most likely to produce happy teachers who are convinced they chose the right career?

4. Which is most likely to produce positive memories for these students twenty years later?

5. Which is most likely to be a positive environment for learning content?

6. Which is most likely to equip a teenager to be a happy and contributing member of the American labor force?

7. Which is most likely to equip a teenager to be a happy and successful college or university student?

8. Which reinforces a student's perception that the large public high school is designed to resemble a warehouse or a factory?

9. Which reinforces a student's perception that high school resembles a four-year prison sentence?

10. Which is most likely to challenge a teenager to improve his or her skills in interpersonal relationships?

11. Which is most likely to enable students to develop, practice, and enhance their inherent potential as leaders?

12. Which is most likely to motivate the teenager contem-

plating career plans to decide, "I believe I want to teach in a high school after I graduate from college?"

From a larger perspective, which of these learning environments is most consistent and compatible with what you believe to be the core purposes of (a) a warehouse, (b) a safe prison, (c) a productive factory, (d) a college preparatory school, or (e) a four-year high school from which fewer than two-thirds of the graduates will complete four years of college?

Notes

Introduction

1. Peter F. Drucker, "Beyond the Information Revolution," *The Atlantic Monthly* (October 1999), 48-50.

2. See Lyle E. Schaller, *Strategies for Change* (Nashville: Abingdon Press, 1993), for a discussion of the importance of discontent in the process of planned change.

1. From Prep School to Prison

1. For a discussion of the wave of indifference and denial initially evoked by Turner's paper, see Ray Allen Billington, *Frederick Jackson Turner* (New York: Oxford University Press, 1993), 184-208.

2. Arthur Meier Schlesinger, *The Rise of the City 1878-1898* (New York: Macmillan, 1933). A forty-two-page chapter is devoted to "The Educational Revival." In it Schlesinger points out that in 1878 two out of five public school teachers were women. Twenty years later, two out of three were female. See p. 167.

3. Edward A. Krug, *The Shaping of the American High School 1880-1920* (Madison: University of Wisconsin Press, 1964), 58-65.

4. Lois Cronholm, "Why One College Jettisoned All Its Remedial Courses," *The Chronicle of Higher Education* (September 24, 1999), B6-B7.

5. Edward A. Krug, *The Shaping of the American High School 1920-1941* (Madison: University of Wisconsin Press, 1972), 7. These two volumes by Professor Krug were essential to recapturing the early decades of the American public high school. Also useful was Joel Spring, *The American School 1642-1993* (New York: McGraw Hill, 1994), and Paul Monroe, *The Founding of the American Public School System* (New York: Macmillan, 1940). A more recent and useful history of the early years of the tax-supported public high school is William Reese, *The Origins of the American High School* (New Haven: Yale University Press, 1995). Reese emphasizes that the early pedagogical methodology emphasized the memorization of facts. The pupils who memorized the most were, by definition, the best educated. That issue continues to be a divisive subject today. Another useful historical account is Arthur Zilversmit, *Changing Schools: Progressive Education Theory and Practice 1930-1960* (Chicago: University of Chicago Press, 1993). The cover conveys the ecological environment of a one-room rural school of the 1930s.

6. Krug, *The Shaping of the American High School 1920-1941*, 313.

7. Ibid., 320.

8. Ibid., 326-27.

9. The concept of the high school as a place of confinement is far from

Notes

new! Back in 1901 Professor Edward A. Ross identified it as "an economical system of police and as the successor to religion as the method of indirect social restraint." Quoted in Thomas Hine, *The Rise and Fall of the American Teenager* (New York: Avon Books, 1999), 155.

10. For a critical view of prison labor, see Gordon Lafer, "Captive Labor: America's Prisoners as Corporate Workforce," *The American Prospect* (September-October 1999), 66-70. For an analysis of the impact on employment, see Bruce Weston and Katherine Beckett, "How Unregulated Is the U.S. Labor Market?" *American Journal of Sociology* (January 1999), 1030-60.

11. Steve Chapman, "The Naked Truth About Keeping Kids Safe at School," *Chicago Tribune* (September 2, 1999).

2. A Century of Explosive Growth

1. Stuart M. Blumin, *The Emergence of the Middle Class* (New York: Cambridge University Press, 1989).

2. Quoted in Edward A. Krug, *The Shaping of the American High School 1880–1920* (Madison: University of Wisconsin Press, 1964), 236.

3. Ibid., 217.

4. Robert H. Wiebe, *The Search for Order* (New York: Hill and Wang, 1967). A superb and provocative discussion of the limitations of the highly centralized command and control system is provided by two retired military officers, Richard A. Gabriel and Paul L. Savage, *Crisis in Command* (New York: Hill and Wang, 1978). One of the dangers they emphasize is when people come to believe leadership and good management are "one and the same thing," 20ff.

5. Raymond E. Callahan, *Education and the Cult of Efficiency* (Chicago: University of Chicago Press, 1962), 237.

6. For explanations on why educational research cannot be expected to drive policy making in education, see D. W. Miller, "The Black Hole of Education Research," *The Chronicle of Higher Education* (August 6, 1999), A17-18. See also Steven Zemelman, Harvey Daniels, and Marilyn Bizar, "Sixty Years of Reading Research—But Who's Listening?" *Phi Delta Kappan* (March 1999), 513-17.

7. Roger G. Barker and Paul V. Gump, *Big School, Small School* (Stanford, Calif.: Stanford University Press, 1964). For a more recent brief summary of the research on the impact of size, see Susan Gallete, "School Size Counts," *Education Digest* (May 1999), 15-17. For a summary of research on class size, see *Reducing Class Size: What Do We Know?* (Washington, D.C.: U.S. Department of Education, March 1999).

3. The Factory Model

1. The use of the factory as a metaphor for the public school surfaces repeatedly in the literature as well as in conversations with students. One recent example is in Sandra Feldman, "Working Together," *The New Republic* (August 30, 1997), 7.

2. Ray Oldenberg, *The Great Good Place* (New York: Paragon Press, 1991).

Notes

4. Does the Environment Matter?

1. Theodore R. Sizer and Nancy Faust Sizer, *The Students Are Watching* (Boston: Beacon Press, 1999), XII.

2. A persuasive argument that the students do possess a unique and extremely valuable perspective is a central theme of *The Students Are Watching*.

3. Roger G. Barker, *Ecological Psychology* (Stanford, Calif.: Stanford University Press, 1968).

4. Seymour B. Sarason, *The Creation of Settings* (San Francisco: Jossey-Bass, 1972).

5. Whether the most productive point of intervention is during the first three years of life or the first six years or the first ten years is not an argument to be pursued here. What most researchers agree on is that the absence of the appropriate intervention during the first twelve years of life places a heavy remedial burden on the contemporary high school. A contrarian view of the importance of the first three years of life is offered by a specialist in neuroscience. See John T. Bruer, *The Myth of the First Three Years: A New Understanding of Early Brain Development and Lifelong Learning* (New York: The Free Press, 1999).

6. This is the central thesis of Sizer and Sizer, *The Students Are Watching*.

7. Massachusetts was the American pioneer in mass public education in the last third of the nineteenth century. An excellent discussion of the role of public schools in assimilating huge numbers of immigrants and of preparing adolescents for life in an industrialized urban society is Marvin Lizerson, *Origins of the Urban School: Public Education in Massachusetts, 1870–1915* (Cambridge, Mass.: Harvard University Press, 1971). The author reports that by 1900 the public high schools in Massachusetts were widely criticized for their incompetence and irrelevance. William Reese, *The Origins of the American High School* (New Haven: Yale University Press, 1995), points out that the early public high schools often were modest enterprises with only one teacher and housed on the third floor or in the attic of a public elementary school.

8. David Tyack and Elisabeth Hansot, *Managers of Virtue* (New York: Basic Books, 1982); Elliott A. Wright, "Religion in American Education: A Historical View," *Phi Delta Kappan* (September 1999), 18.

9. These three paragraphs draw heavily on Raymond E. Callahan, *The Cult of Efficiency* (Chicago: University of Chicago Press, 1962). In 1914–15 the Gary public school system pioneered the "released time" concept, which enabled students to be dismissed from school to go to a nearby church or synagogue for religious instruction. See Wright, "Religion in American Education," 17-20.

10. Near the end of the 1995 motion picture *Mr. Holland's Opus*, the governor makes a powerful statement about the most important criterion for the evaluation of a teacher. She declares that helping teenagers learn to excel in at least one area of life is that criterion, not his fame as a composer, for evaluating Glen Holland's career. The central theme of the movie is about adults helping teenagers excel in what they have never done and know they cannot do.

Notes

11. This observer's earlier reflections on the importance of place were delivered in the H. Paul Douglass lecture of 1974. See Lyle E. Schaller, *Effective Church Planning* (Nashville: Abingdon Press, 1979), 65-92. For a sociolegal perspective, see Patricia Ewick and Susan S. Silbey, *The Common Place of Law* (Chicago: University of Chicago Press, 1999). For a discussion of the impact of the electronic media on social behavior, see Joshua Meyrowitz, *No Sense of Place* (New York: Oxford University Press, 1985).

12. Quoted in Asa Briggs, "The Sense of Place," in The Smithsonian Annual II, *The Fitness of Man's Environment* (Washington, D.C.: Smithsonian Institution Press, 1968), 83.

13. H. G. Bissenger, *Friday Night Lights* (Reading, Mass.: Addison-Wesley, 1990), 42-43.

14. Ray Oldenberg, *The Great Good Place* (New York: Paragon Press, 1991).

15. The tendency of human beings to engage in violent behavior is discussed in Nancy Brener et al., "Recent Trends in Violence-Related Behavior Among High School Students in the United States," *Journal of the American Medical Association* (August 4, 1999), 440-45; Timothy Quinnan, "Preparing for the Moment When a Student's Rage Turns to Violence," *The Chronicle of Higher Education* (August 22, 1999), 30-41; Ann Rule, *A Rage to Kill* (New York: Pocket Star, 1999); Larry Doyle, "Killers Among Us," *New York Times Magazine*, August 22, 1999, 13-14; Stephen S. Hall, "The Bully in the Mirror," *New York Times Magazine*, August 22, 1999, 30-41. Perhaps the most persuasive argument of how the ecological environment can influence both attitudes and behavior is told by a journalist who spent a year as a guard in Sing Sing Prison in New York. This book explains how the environment can encourage both inmates and guards to engage in extreme forms of antisocial behavior. Ted Conover, *New Jack* (New York: Random House, 2000).

16. For a discussion on the role of discontent and conflict in promoting change, see Lyle E. Schaller, *Community Organization: Conflict and Reconciliation* (Nashville: Abingdon Press, 1966), 72-114.

17. For a thoughtful explanation of this subject by a high school student in Littleton, Colorado, see Nathan Black, "Yes, I'm in a Clique," *The New York Times*, April 29, 1999.

18. Stan Friedland, "Less Violence? Change the School Culture," *The Education Digest* (September 1999), 6-9.

19. A provocative and thoughtful analysis of the charter schools in ten California districts is Amy Stuart Wells, Alejandra Lopez, Janelle Scott, and Jennifer Jellison Holme, "Charter Schools as Postmodern Paradox: Rethinking Social Stratification in the Age of Deregulated School Choice," *Harvard Educational Review* (summer 1999), 172-204.

6. Is It a Dysfunctional System?

1. Redding S. Sugg, Jr., *Mother Teacher: The Feminization of American Education* (Charlottesville: University of Virginia Press, 1978), 18-39.

2. For another brief discussion on this point, see James Heaney, "Easy Pickings," *The Washington Monthly* (May 1997), 24-25.

Notes

3. Mary A. Carskadon, "When Worlds Collide," *Phi Delta Kappan* (January 1999), 348-52; Kyla L. Wahlstrom, "The Prickly Politics of School Starting Times," *Phi Delta Kappan* (January 1999), 345-47.

4. See note 10 to chapter 4. Mr. Holland's reward for thirty years of helping students learn to excel was the elimination of his position as a music teacher.

5. Paul C. Vitz, "Cupid's Broken Arrow," *Phi Delta Kappan* (March 1999), 547.

6. The tendency to overload teachers with an excessively long set of expectations is pointed out in "The U.S. Education System: Overview of the Current Environment," *Congressional Digest* (August-September 1999), 197.

7. This is the dilemma in which the United States military organizations find themselves. What is their primary function? To win battles? To educate high school dropouts? To police places such as Kosovo or Haiti? To provide disaster relief? To provide scholarships to enable young adults to go to college? To reduce racial discrimination in American society? To train pilots for the commercial airlines?

8. John W. Appel, "Fighting Fear," *American Heritage* (October 1999), 26.

9. Ibid., 28-29.

7. What Day Is It?

1. One outstanding example of this was the "Port Huron Statement" adopted in 1962 by a few dozen members of Students For a Democratic Society. See Alan Adelson, *SDS* (New York: Charles Scribner's Sons, 1972), 206-8.

2. Peter Beinart, "The Rise of Jewish Schools," *The Atlantic Monthly* (October 1999), 21-22.

3. Jacques Steinberg, "Schools Ceding College Placement to Consultants," *New York Times,* (September 5, 1999), A12.

8. What Happened to the Post Office?

1. For an earlier introduction to this debate, see *The Public School Monopoly,* ed. Robert B. Everhart (San Francisco: Pacific Institute for Public Policy Research, 1982).

2. The difficulty of identifying the growing support for vouchers as a "liberal" or "conservative" movement was illustrated in the summer of 1999. In June an elementary school principal came out in support of vouchers to enable parents to send their children to a private school as part of a larger strategy to enhance competition. See Michael Mote, "Going All the Way," *Phi Delta Kappan* (June 1999), 466-69. A few weeks later, Marv Knox, editor of the largest regional newspaper in the Southern Baptist Convention, came out strongly in opposition and urged Christians to continue sending their children to public schools. See Marv Knox, "Exodus Could Balkanize America," *Baptist Standard* (August 18, 1999). A week later, a liberal weekly published a long essay by a notable social activist advocating that educational reform efforts must include family choice, including vouchers. See Ronald J. Sider, "Making Schools Work for the Rich and the Poor," *Christian Century* (August 25-September 1, 1999), 802-9. Two weeks later, a British newsmagazine in its

Notes

American edition carried an editorial endorsement of vouchers for private (but not religious) schools as the "second best" alternative. See "America's Vouchers Battle," *The Economist* (September 4, 1999), 26-27.

3. Clarence Page, "Resistance to School Vouchers by African-Americans Is Starting to Change," *The Chicago Tribune*, May 23, 1999. Another perspective is offered by former Democratic member of Congress and current senior pastor of a black megachurch, Floyd H. Flake, "School Choice: Why Poor Kids Need It Most of All," *American Experiment Quarterly* (spring 1999), 35-42.

9. Ten Public Policy Questions

1. For a more skeptical view of what can be expected of parents, see Chester E. Finn, Jr., "Can Parents Be Trusted?" *Commentary* (September 1999), 45-52. This observer is more optimistic if the ecological environment can be transformed to include greater trust in parents.

2. P. J. Simmons, "Learning to Live with NGOs," *Foreign Policy* (fall 1999), 82-86.

3. An excellent analysis of this partnership to implement the welfare-to-work program is Peter Frumkin and Alice Andrew-Clark, "The Rise of the Corporate Social Worker," *Society* (September/October 1999), 46-52. For another perspective on whether for-profit corporations threaten the future of nonprofit organizations, see William P. Rajan, "The New Landscape for Nonprofits," *Harvard Business Review* (January-February 1999), 127-36.

4. For-profit postsecondary school institutions have been around for decades but in recent years have expanded rapidly. In 1997, for example, the University of Phoenix, with 60,000 students, produced a profit of $33 million. For an analysis for an economics as well as a public-policy perspective, see Gordon C. Winston, "For-Profit Higher Education: Godzilla or Chicken Little?" *Change* (January/February 1999), 13-19.

5. For an early analysis of the impact of the competition, see Richard Arum, "Do Private Schools Force Public Schools to Compete?" *American Sociological Review* 61, 1 (February 1996), 29-46.

6. For this section I am indebted to Lloyd P. Jorgenson, *The State and the Non-Public School 1825–1925* (Columbia: University of Missouri Press, 1987). This is a superb review of the growth of the Common School movement as a response to the widespread fear that Roman Catholic schools were a threat to republican institutions.

7. An excellent summary of the Australian experience is Anthony Potts, "Public and Private Schooling in Australia," *Phi Delta Kappan* (November 1999), 242-45.

10. What Do They Do Best?

1. Francis A. J. Ianni, *The Search for Structure: A Report on American Youth Today* (New York: The Free Press, 1989).

2. Julianne Basinger, "Colleges Experiment With Charter Schools," *The Chronicle of Higher Education* (October 29, 1999), A51.

Notes

11. Six Pressures for Radical Change

1. This is far from a new insight! A useful introductory history of the efforts and failure to change the old educational environment is Zilversmit, *Changing Schools.* A brief introduction to this issue can be found on pages 83-89.

2. Sandra Feldman, "Where We Stand," *The New Republic* (August 30, 1999), 7.

3. This section was informed by the reading of Gerald Grant and Christine E. Murray, *Teaching in America: The Slow Revolution* (Cambridge, Mass.: Harvard University Press, 1999). This book should be required reading by anyone interested in implementing the proposal by Sandra Feldman that teachers be identified as members of a profession. From this observer's perspective, it ranks up there with Vivian Gussin Paley, *You Don't Say You Can't Play* (Cambridge, Mass.: Harvard University Press, 1992) and the books by Sizer and Sizer and Bassinger cited earlier as essential reading for anyone who wants to look at the world through the eyes of the student or the teacher.

Those who are convinced there is a future for university-based colleges of education will be stimulated by John I. Goodlad, "Rediscovering Teacher Education: School Renewal and Educating Educators," *Change* (September/October 1999), 29-33. Goodlad lifts up the consequences when a professional school identifies itself as a research center rather than a place to equip practitioners. See also Ted Hipple, "It's Elementary: Better Training, Better Teachers," *Chronicle of Higher Education* (July 30, 1999), B6.

4. The Milton Hershey School was founded in 1909 for the "maintenance, support and education" of poor orphan boys. Ninety years later the endowment fund has grown to $5 billion, and the school was spending an average of $60,000 annually for each of the 1,060 disadvantaged students.

5. Jack Wertheimer, "Who's Afraid of Jewish Day Schools?" *Commentary* (December 1999), 49-53. Wertheimer states that 700 Jewish day schools currently enroll 200,000 pupils K-12.

6. One reason to suggest the United States Marine Corps as a source of useful lessons is their success in transforming recruits, many of whom come from the bottom half of the socio-economic ladder of American society, into skilled, self-confident, reliable, and proud Marines. See Thomas E. Ricks, *Making the Corps* (New York: Scribner, 1997). Those who are worried about the use of a military model will find support for their concern in the 1990–99 survey by the Triangle Institute for Security Studies. Adam Clymer, "Sharp Divergence Found in Views of Military and Civilians," *New York Times,* September 9, 1999.

12. What Is a Learning Community?

1. For a brief introduction to a person many believe to be the most effective mentor in the modern history of the Western world, see the review by Sherwin B. Nuland of the book Michael Bliss, *William Osler: A Life in Medicine* (New York: Oxford University Press, 1999) in *The New Republic* (December 13, 1999), 27-33.